INSIDE CHURCHES

A Guide to Church Furnishings

Based on the original edition by Patricia Dirsztay

NADFAS

NATIONAL ASSOCIATION OF DECORATIVE & FINE ARTS SOCIETIES

© National Association of Decorative & Fine Arts Societies 1993

First edition 1989

Revised edition 1993
In association with NADFAS Church Recorders
Based on the original edition by Patricia Dirsztay

Revised edition 2001 published by NADFAS Enterprises Limited
NADFAS House, 8 Guilford Street, London WC1N 1DA
Telephone: (020) 7430 0730 Fax: (020) 7242 0686
E-mail: nel@nadfas.org.uk

Revised typesetting: Peter Constable Consultants Limited
Cover design and print management: Siân Cardy
Printing: Gemini Press

A CIP catalogue record for this book is available from the British Library

ISBN 0 9540191 0 5

INSIDE CHURCHES has been compiled by the National Association of Decorative & Fine Arts Societies who would like to acknowledge with thanks the generous help and advice of the following:

Michael Archer†; David Beasley, Librarian, Goldsmiths' Hall; Jennifer Beazley*; Margaret Bell; John Blair, The Queens College, Oxford; Chris Blanchett, Tiles & Architectural Ceramics Society; Sheila Chapman*; Pamela Clabburn,textile & embroidery consultant; RWM Clouston; Gerald Cole*; Pamela Cowen; Barbara Crow*; Patricia Dirsztay; Elizabeth Eames; Donald Findlay•; Philippa Glanville, Director, Waddesdon Manor, Herts; Angela Goedicke*; Richard Grasby†; Linda Hall†; Hugh Harrison; Dr Mary Hobbs•; Dr Doris Jones-Baker; Dr Brian Kemp, Church Monuments Society; Sheelagh Lewis†; Joyce Little*; Nick Norman•; Dr Tony North, Assistant Curator, Metalwork Collection, Victoria & Albert Museum; Ian Pickford†; Dr John Richardson, The Pewter Society; Tom Robinson, Chairman, The Antiquarian Horological Society; the Rev Richard Robson; Madeau Stewart; Elliott Viney; Lt Col JF Willcocks†, NADFAS Heraldry Adviser; Dr Donald Wright, British Institute of Organ Studies; Doreen Yarwood•.

Drawings: Caroline Cook; Frances Curwen; Marilyn Lane; Paul Vincent; Doreen Yarwood.

Revision: Indexing, proof reading and production: Angela Goedicke, Patricia Braun and Jill Hardie-Bick

* member of NADFAS Church Recorders
† NADFAS lecturer
• deceased

PREFACE

The Most Reverend George Carey, Archbishop of Canterbury

It is one of the privileges of my ministry to worship in many beautiful cathedrals and parish churches. They are almost always cared for lovingly. But I am conscious that we should not take our inheritance of historic buildings for granted. As social needs change and our communities become more mobile parish churches become more vulnerable. Most communities know more or less what their church looks like, but even the most committed members of the parish may be surprisingly unaware of the significance of the decoration and the furniture which their church contains. It is not just that churches are places of peace and beauty, but also that they have so much to tell us of our own history.

This book will help all of us to interpret that history. Its publication celebrates the work of the Church Recorders of the National Association of Decorative and Fine Arts Societies and marks their Twentieth Anniversary. For twenty years, small groups of amateur enthusiasts have been painstakingly recording every item of furniture and interior decoration in parish churches, large and small, all over the country. Their efforts form the only national inventory of the contents of our hundreds of churches today. The importance of this Record for the future conservation and preservation of churches cannot be overestimated; without it we should have very little idea of where to start.

I congratulate the Church Recorders on twenty valuable years' dedication to the conservation of our churches. Perhaps we should also congratulate them for sharing their knowledge in making this book available, so that we all have an opportunity to understand and enjoy what we see around us in our churches.

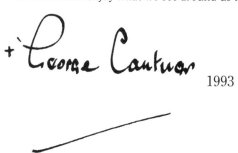

1993

CONTENTS

CONTENTS

CONTENTS

AN INTRODUCTION TO THE HISTORY OF THE CHURCH IN BRITAIN

Churches in Britain encapsulate much of the complex history of these islands. Nearly every town and village has its own parish church and most often it is the oldest building, set apart from the dwellings of ordinary people. Many churches are truly ancient, the first buildings in stone by early Christians, dating back to a time when religion was the main spring of society. It is not uncommon to find a church built by the Norman settlers of the 11th century but it is unusual for any church to date from only one century; many have something to offer from every period of our history. From the start, the shape, decoration and furnishings of our cathedrals and parish churches have been governed by the services held in them.

Although there has been a constant evolution over the centuries, we can recognise three distinct periods: the six hundred years to the Reformation in the mid-16th century; the next three hundred years during which a whole series of fundamental changes were followed by a period of stagnation; and finally a re-awakening from the 1840's to today.

The Medieval Centuries

The entire medieval period was dominated by its religion and it is easy to forget that medieval religion was international, based on a complex ritual centred on the Pope in Rome. Early churches were, therefore, Roman Catholic.

The Anglo-Saxons can have had few furnishings in their places of worship, apart from the cup used at Mass. From the earliest times, there would have been a font for baptism and, because it is usually free-standing, the font has often survived from Norman times even if the church around it has been entirely rebuilt. The Normans built many small stone 3 or 4 cell churches with a small chancel and a slightly larger nave. In the earliest, processions around a tomb of a saint or bishop were an essential part of ritual and a rounded apse at the east end of the church provided space. As churches increased in size, the aisles took over this function and the east end tended to be flattened.

The 11th and 12th centuries were the great period of monasticism. Many churches were bequeathed by their lay patrons to a wealthy cathedral or abbey. From earliest times, the chancel had been the responsibility of the priest and the nave of the parish. With the appointment of church wardens from 1129, the laiety had more influence on changes in the main body of the church. The patronage of wealthy benefactors encouraged a proliferation of new aisles, steeples, porches, towers and clerestory windows all of which fundamentally affected the appearance of the church.

The 12th and 15th centuries saw a period of extraordinary decorative innovation. Perhaps the most significant was the arrival of stained glass, in cathedrals from the 1170's and in parish churches in the 13th century. At the same time wall paintings began to appear, covering the nave walls with biblical scenes and always focused on the great Doom or Day of Judgement over the chancel and above the rood. In the 13th century mass would have been said daily. A traveller entering the south door would have first seen the figure of St Christopher painted on the opposite wall. The single Sanctus bell would have told him that the service was starting; it would have rung again at the Elevation of the Host. Mass could only be said once daily at any particular altar, so as the number of priests grew, it became necessary to have additional altars, often placed at the east end of the side-aisles, so that separate chapels within the main body of the church were formed.

Not many medieval churches had pulpits. Preaching was more often done by friars at the village cross which could be in the churchyard or on the village green. In the 13th century, fonts were covered to protect the consecrated water from theft. It seems that the consecrated water was seldom changed.

Memorials began to appear. For centuries they were confined to the graves of priests and great men. At first, even the grandest had only a simple cross incised on their tomb slabs. These developed into figures of recumbent knights and ladies, first in stone and then in alabaster. The less ambitious or those who could not afford a massive stone or marble monument were content with a decorated brass memorial. The earliest brass in England is dated 1277 and they continued to be popular until the early 17th century.

The Black Death, or bubonic plague, that swept the country in the mid-14th century was a social and economic disaster but it had another long term effect in encouraging a general acceptance of the uncertainty of life and an increasing concern for the after-life. The wealthy began to build chantry chapels, endowing them with a priest to pray perpetually for their souls. The obsession with death can be seen in the skulls and skeletons carved into monuments.

In the century before the Reformation, there was much rebuilding, particularly in the counties which prospered from the wool trade, but everywhere towers were being added to the west end of churches. These were principally to house a set of bells, but there was undoubtedly rivalry between neighbouring parishes to build the grandest or the highest tower. Two other developments mark the 15th century. The introduction of simple benches for seating and the substitution of the old steep pitched roof by a flatter one which made possible the insertion of a new tier of clerestory windows high above the nave.

The Anglican Church

The immediate effect of the Reformation in the 1530's was devastating. The new religion was based on preaching and the community and its churches were plain and unadorned; the colourful arenas of the medieval saints were no longer acceptable.

An obsession with idolatry meant the destruction of almost all visible decoration. Wall paintings were whitewashed, fonts and monuments defaced, stone altars and the rood removed, plate and vestments confiscated and much stained glass destroyed. For the first time, laymen could enter the chancel whether the dividing rood screen had been destroyed or not. A new wooden Holy Table took the place of the stone altar.

To accommodate the changed needs of the changed liturgy, in the 17th century, a number of new furnishings appeared. The new Anglican service emphasised Mattins and Evensong so the Eucharist or communion mass became an occasional service. Since preaching was the most important element of these services, for the next two hundred years the pulpit was the dominant feature in most churches. Pulpits were set high because they had to place the preacher above the new box pews and the tester above helped to carry the preacher's words to the ends of the church.

Other innovations of these years were the Poorbox and the Breadbasket for the distribution of alms to the poor, based on the medieval monastic system of Bread Dole. The display of The Sentences (Lord's Prayer, Creed and Ten Commandments), made obligatory in churches in 1603, and the Royal Arms, signifying the monarch as Head of the Church, became a universal ornament after 1662. In the 1630's, Archbishop Laud introduced altar rails to prevent dogs from approaching the Table.

Almost no new churches were built between the Reformation and the Great Fire of London after which a radically different style of church design appeared, classical in form and planned to accommodate the contemporary liturgy. Architects like Wren, Hawksmoor and Gibbs saw churches as preaching boxes, rectangular halls with galleries, plain glass in round-headed windows, no east window but a reredos behind the altar, probably incorporating the Sentences, box pews and a dominating pulpit. Magnificent new plate was donated by patrons and, in country churches, hatchments were set high on the walls when the local squire died. This was the great age of English sculpture and magnificent, but often overlarge, monuments filled the chancel.

The Victorian Revival and After

The Church of England dozed through the late 18th and early 19th centuries, leaving churches generally damp, decaying and uncared for until the electric impact of the Oxford Movement in the 1840's jerked the Church out of its inertia. With the Ecclesiologists in command, there began a revolution which, in 30 years, restored or built the majority of parish churches, saving many from total decay but destroying or distorting much of beauty and antiquity in the process. A reaction against the Carolean and Georgian periods meant the loss of box pews and many pulpits and the removal of classical monuments to more obscure parts of the building. The musicians in the west gallery were replaced by a surpliced choir in the chancel backed by an organ. There were new brass lecterns, altarcloths, vestments, new tiles on the floor and new stained glass (of very varying quality) in the windows. Pulpits were rebuilt in stone and fonts, which had become much smaller after the Reformation when total immersion at baptism ceased, returned to their medieval size.

There have been changes enough since then. Today's churches offer us a mix and amalgam of all periods and architectural styles. Search for it and there is evidence to be found of every period of the church's gradual evolution. Radical changes in belief and liturgy produced sudden new directions. We can trace them through the objects, decoration and furnishings they left behind. It is the sheer variety of Britain's churches and the historical breadth that they incorporate that combines to ensure their perennial fascination.

How to Use This Guide

Inside Churches is a practical reference book. It will help you to name and identify the furnishings of any parish church or cathedral in Britain. This is how it works....

At the front is a **general introduction** to the history of the church in Britain from earliest times until today. The book is organised in three overall sections:

Styles and Terminology chapters will tell you HOW to describe the things you see

Materials chapters will tell you WHAT you see depending whether it is made of wood, metal, paper, cloth or stone

Objects chapters will tell you WHAT it is if it falls into one of several special categories; clocks; memorials and monuments; musical instruments; windows

Sections are divided into chapters and chapters into sub-sections dealing with specific groups of styles or objects.

If, for example, you are looking at a piece of furniture. Is it made of wood? Turn to the MATERIALS section then to the WOOD chapter. At the beginning of the chapter you find a glossary of the special terms used to describe types of wood and types of decoration and construction specific to this material. If your piece of furniture looks like a table, turn to the sub-section TABLES. Does it look like any of the illustrated examples? If so, you will find either its name and, perhaps, date or even a full description of it using the correct terms. If you can find no similar illustration, turn back to the front of the chapter to identify its constituent parts (legs, feet and backs give the most clues). Turn to the STYLES AND TERMINOLOGY section for information on the decoration and date.

Using the book, you will have found out exactly what it is, what it was used for, approximately how old it might be and how to describe it. If you already know what the object is but want to learn more, or if you come across a term that is unfamiliar, turn to the **Index** in the back of the book.

Throughout the text, proper names are in bold thus

descriptions are in roman type, thus

and explanations are in brackets in italic type, thus

Credence

of trestle form

(sanctuary table)

Inside Churches primary aim is to help people record the objects and decoration in churches. CHURCH RECORDERS will find notes in italics at the foot of those sections where particular recording techniques are advised. In general, however, you will need to describe the object in detail noting decoration, colour, position, inscriptions or maker's name and its state of preservation. Add photographs and sketch drawings where you can.

For more information on Church Recorders, write to: **Church Recorders, The National Association of Decorative and Fine Arts Societies, NADFAS House, 8 Guilford Street, London WC1N 1DA.**

Inside Churches will give you an introduction to a wide number of decorative and fine arts and help increase your knowledge of church interiors. However, it would not be practical to answer all your questions, so if you want to know more about any particular aspect, turn to FURTHER READING for a selection of reference books.

STYLES & TERMINOLOGY

ARCHITECTURE
Terms

The main decorative periods of British Church Art and Architecture are:

650-1050	Saxon
1050-1200	Romanesque (Norman)
1175-1550	**GOTHIC**
1175-1300	Early English
1300-1380	Decorated
1380-1550	Perpendicular
1550-1600	Elizabethan
1600-1650	Early Stuart
1650-1670	Artisan Mannerist
1670-1690	Restoration
1690-1720	Baroque
1720-1830	**GEORGIAN**
1720-1760	Palladian
1760-1790	Neoclassical
1790-1830	Regency
1830-1890	Victorian
1890-1920	Arts and Crafts
	Art Nouveau
1920-1940	Art Deco
	Thirties
1950-1965	Modernist
1965-1980	Brutalist
1980-	Post-Modern

THE CHURCH

Christian churches are most often cruciform in shape with the altar at the eastern end.

2

Lugged or eared architrave

ABACUS
The slab on top of a **capital** on which the **architrave** rests; the shape varies according to the **Order**

ARCHITRAVE
The moulded frame surrounding a door or window. It is also the lowest main division of the **entablature**, between the **frieze** and **abacus**. A **lintel** is the horizontal member over a door or window

CORNICE
The uppermost member of a entablature, surmounting the frieze, or any moulded projection which crowns the part to which it is fixed, eg. wall, door, column, piece of furniture, window, panelling, etc

FRIEZE
A decorative band between the architrave and cornice or, in furniture, between the cornice and framework

IMPOST
The slab, usually moulded, on which the ends of an **arch** rest

PEDIMENT
An ornamental low pitched triangular or segmental gable above the cornice of an entablature

Triangular   Segmental   Swan-necked

Broken   Open   Scrolled

Spur

SPUR
An ornamental protrusion on the corner between the base of a **column** or **pillar** and the **plinth**. Also a fixed draught **screen**, or a **buttress**

TYMPANUM
The filled-in space of a pediment or of the curved section of an arch

3

ARCHITECTURE
Terms

Cornice
Frieze
Architrave — **Entablature**

Abacus
Capital

COLUMNS
The horizontal members above a column resting on the abacus *(which is part of the capital).* Parts of an entablature may also be on a wall or other structure without columnar support

Shaft

Base

Plinth

Doric frieze with **mutules** *(projecting brackets)* above **triglyphs** *(grooved tablets)* alternating with **metopes** *(square spaces)* here containing bucrania and with **guttae** *(drops)* below, also found on monuments (see page 57)

Ionic Capital
with angle volutes

BASES
Attic Base
scotia *(concave moulding)* between two **tori** *(large convex mouldings)*

Tuscan Base
torus with a fillet above (see page 92)

Base
with two **astragals** *(small convex moulding)* with a scotia above and a torus below

- Crown with Lantern
- Lunette in Dome which rises from a Drum
- Modillions (see page 7)
- Pediment with Escutcheon in the Tympanum
- Balustrade
- Portico
- Plinth

ARCADE
A series of arches supported on piers or columns

Hatchment in **Spandrel**

Respond *(a half pillar or shaft engaged with a wall to support an arch, usually at the end of an arcade)*

Dado rail returned, continuing at right angles along the end wall

Acroterion ornament at apex or lower angles of pediment
Stylobate continuous base supporting a colonnade

ARCHITECTURE
Columns and Supports

The term **column** in classical architecture is an upright structural member of round or polygonal section with a shaft, a capital and usually, a base. The term **pillar** is used in Gothic architecture (see page 7).

DORIC
is distinguished by triglyphs and metopes in the frieze and mutules under the corona
Greek Doric has a fluted shaft and no base
Roman Doric has an attic base and fluted or plain shaft

IONIC
has volutes on the capital and dentils in the cornice, a fluted shaft and an attic base

CORINTHIAN
has a fluted shaft, a capital ornamented with acanthus, olive or laurel leaves, eight small volutes and an attic base

TUSCAN
is simplified Doric

COMPOSITE
is an ornate version of Corinthian and occurs in various forms

Doric Ionic Corinthian Tuscan Composite

OTHER CAPITALS

 Cushion Norman

 Scalloped Norman

 Waterleaf 12th century

 Crocket Transitional

 Stiff Leaf 13th century

 Natural Leaf 14th century

**Engaged
Column**

**Pilaster
Strip**
*(thin pilaster
without base
or capital)*

Colonnettes
*(diminutive
columns)*

**Compound
Pier**
*(a solid core
surrounded by
attached or
detached
shafts)*

Pillar
*(solid detached
upright support
in Gothic
architecture)*

Modillion
*(small
projecting
console
brackets
under the
eaves)*

Blind Arcade

**Pillar of clustered
shafts**
*(often misnamed as
clustered column)*

Pilaster
*(flat representation of
a classical column in
shallow relief against
a wall)*

Colonnade

ARCHITECTURE
Arches

1 Structure of an arch

A Keystone   F Soffit
B Voussoir   G Impost
C Springer   H Springing Line
D Intrados   I Rise
E Extrados   J Span

An **arch** is a structure of wedge-shaped blocks of stone, brick or concrete covering an opening which support one another by mutual pressure and are thus capable of carrying considerable weight (1)

The Etruscans constructed arches composed of radiating blocks (**voussoirs**); a number of examples survive in town gateways of central Italy as at Volterra. The Romans then adapted this method of construction extensively in order to suit their more complex needs (2)

The classical arch, whether ancient Roman, Renaissance or Modern is, therefore, round-headed as is also the Romanesque (Norman) design which, as the name suggests, is derived from Rome (3, 4)

The most important feature of Gothic architecture, introduced in the late 12th century, was the pointed arch or, as the French aptly term it, the **arc brisé**

The early form was narrow and sharply pointed, the **lancet** or Early English shape (6)

2 Arch of Titus, Rome AD 81

3 Romanesque doorway 1170

8 Four-centred arched gateway 1510

7 Ogee arched doorway 1360

4 Classical doorway 1713-14

6 Lancet window opening 1204

5 Gothic doorway (equilateral arch) c1300

Gradually the arch widened to the equilateral form where height was equal to width. Later variations included, for example, the ogee with its double curve form, concave to convex (7) and the late medieval four-centred shape of two different convex curves (8)

Drawings by Doreen Yarwood *Chronology of Western Architecture*, Batsford

AEDICULE

A classical architectural surround to an opening *(door, window, niche, etc)* composed of columns and an entablature, sometimes with a pediment

Pediment with Escutcheon in Tympanum

Cornice
Frieze
Architrave

Soffit *(underside of lintel or arch)*

Niche with splayed jambs

Sill

Apron   Bracket

Pedestal

Surbase

Plinth

Embrasure (spaces)
Merlon (projections)
Crown *(top of the arch)*
Embattled

Haunch
Quatrefoil in Tympanum
Hood-mould or dripstone
Soffit *(under side of the arch)*
Stop
Springing
Trumeau
(supports tympanum)

ARCHITECTURE
Timber Trussed Roofs

Such open roofs, constructed of massive timbers, were developed from the early Middle Ages and covered many church roof interiors until the early 20th century. The word **truss** is given to the system of timbers, each of which was tenoned and pegged to provide a stable structure which would resist all thrusts. In general, the medieval roof was gabled at each end with a fairly steep pitch. A long beam, the **ridge pole** or **piece**, extended horizontally along the apex from one end of the roof to the other. Further beams, the **purlins**, were set at intervals parallel to the ridge pole and at the top edge of the walls were placed very heavy beams called **wall plates**, supported by stone **corbels**. At right angles to these timbers were fixed the rafters which extended from wall plate to ridge. The simplest truss was developed early in the Middle Ages. This was the tie beam structure. In this a massive beam was thrown across the nave or choir at wall plate level to counteract the outward thrust of the roof upon the walls. On this tie beam was generally set a central vertical post rising from tie beam to ridge pole, a **king post**. Sometimes a pair of such posts were used, **queen posts**. Alternatively a **crown post** was used, in this case a vertical post extended from the centre of the tie beam to a higher horizontal beam, the **collar beam**. In all cases straight struts and curved braces were introduced as reinforcement was needed.

1 Timber trussed roof

A	Ridge-piece
B	Rafter
C	Principal rafter
D	Purlin
E	Wall plate
F	Tie beam
G	King post
H	Brace

3
A Collar purlin
B Crown post
C Collar beam
D Tie beam

2 Collar beam roof
A Wall plate
B Purlin
C Principal rafters
D Arch brace
E Collar beam

4 Hammer-beam roof
Westminster Hall

5 Double Hammer-beam roof
A Hammer beam
B Hammer post
C Corbel
D Arch brace
E Wall post
F Purlin
G Principal rafter
H Collar beam

Drawings by Doreen Yarwood. *English Interiors* Lutterworth Press

A later, more complex, phase could be seen in the **hammerbeam** roof design which was developed in the late 14th century. Hammerbeams resembled cut-off tie beams. They extended at wall plate level and were supported from corbels by arch-braced wall posts: both corbels and hammerbeam ends were generally decoratively carved. The shorter hammerbeams gave better visibility than the tie beams and reduced lateral pressure. Vertical hammer posts rose from the inner end of the hammerbeams to a collar beam above or to a second hammerbeam.

The sanctuary is the focal point of the church. Although its arrangement is not strictly architectural much architectural terminology is used to describe it. The arrangement will differ according to the form of the service. In Anglican churches, the Sacrament will generally be kept in an **aumbry** or **hanging pyx**. In Roman Catholic churches, the Sacrament is generally kept in a **tabernacle** on the altar.

E
N—|— S
W
Sanctuary lamp

Reredos (here, a triptych)

Gradine

Superfrontal
Alms dish
Credence

Frontal
Footpace

Altar	elevated slab or wooden table used for the celebration of Holy Communion
Antependium	movable panel of carved or painted wood or metal serving as a front cover for the altar
Aumbry	two accepted uses: first, a recessed cupboard in the wall of a church (anywhere in the building, for any use) and secondly the specific use of such a cupboard, normally on the north side of the high altar or Lady Chapel altar, as a place in which the Blessed Sacrament is reserved
Credence	table or shelf on south side of the altar used for the sacra-mental elements and vessels during Communion Services
Footpace	step on which the altar stands, returning to the East wall rather than running across the sanctuary
Frontal	textile forming covering for the front of an altar
Gradine	shelf at rear of the altar top, sometimes attached to the Reredos
Laudian frontal	loose three or four-sided throw-over altar covering reaching to the ground on all sides
Predella	a subsidary panel or series of panels, below the main representation in an altarpiece or a stained glass window
Reredos	fixed screen behind and above the altar: **Altarpiece**, if it is a painting; **Dossal**, if it is a curtain; **Diptych** (two panels) or **Triptych** (three panels), if a hinged painting or panel
Superfrontal	band of material, usually fringed and sometimes contrasting, overlapping the upper edge of the frontal
Tabernacle	receptacle for the Reserved Sacrament. A box-like structure placed in the centre of the altar and generally used in Roman Catholic churches

ATTRIBUTES AND ALLEGORY
Saints

Biblical stories depicted in stained glass, sculpture and painted scenes had to be understood by people who could not read. Through the medieval period a complex iconography developed linking every saint, apostle or biblical personality with an image which identified him with the event that gave him prominence. Today, these images are often incomprehensible because we no longer understand the references.

SAINTS' ATTRIBUTES

Images of Saints were easily identified by medieval people by the symbols or attributes they carried. A woman holding a wheel, for example, is probably Catherine of Alexandria who was martyred on a wheel.

Saints usually have more than one attribute and the combination of several helps to identify them. A dragon, for example, is associated with several saints, but one next to, or below, a winged figure (often in armour) identifies St Michael, whereas one associated with a knight without wings will identify St George. Attributes are not depicted consistently in the same way, eg St Ursula sometimes holds an arrow and is sometimes pierced by one.

Saints are listed first by attribute and then by name. Their accustomed dress is not strictly an attribute, but is included as one where appropriate since it may be an important identifying characteristic.

BEASTS AND MEN

Cow	Bridgit of Kildare
Does (2)	Withburga
Dog	Roch, with plague sore on leg
Dogs (2)	Dominic, with black and white dogs holding torches in mouths
Dragon & cross	Margaret of Antioch
Dragon	Archangel Michael (winged); George, usually in armour;
Dragon led by chain	Juliana of Nicanedia
Dragon led by rope or ribbon	Martha
Horse, white	George
Lamb	Agnes; Francis of Assisi; John the Baptist
Lion & raven	Vincent of Sarogossa
Lion (winged)	Mark
Lion	Euphemia or Jerome
Man (winged)	Matthew
Mule (kneeling)	Anthony of Padua

Otter	Bishop Cuthbert
Ox (winged)	Luke
Oxen (2)	Walstan, who also holds scythe
Pig, boar or hog	Anthony of Egypt (Anthony Abbot)
Sheep	Genevieve
Stag (crucifix between horns)	Eustace or Hubert
Wolf (guarding head)	Edmund
Wolf, Lion or Cock	Vitus

BIRDS

Birds	Francis of Assisi
Cock	Peter
Cock, lion or wolf	Vitus
Dove on sceptre	King Edmund
Dove on shoulder	David of Wales
Dove	Pope Gregory
Doves in cage or basket (2)	Joseph or Joachim
Eagle	John the Evangelist
Swan & flowers	Hugh of Lincoln

OBJECTS AND FLOWERS

Anchor	Clement or Nicholas of Myra
Anvil	Adrian or Bishop Eloi
Armour (winged with dragon)	Michael
Armour (no wings and with dragon)	George
Arrow (in hand)	Ursula
Arrow (piercing breast or hand)	Giles
Arrow	Edmund
Arrows (pierced by and bound to tree or column)	Sebastian (naked)
Axe	Matthias
Axe (in head)	Peter the Martyr
Bag of money	Matthew or Judas Iscariot
Balls (3)	Nicholas of Myra
Banner (red cross & surrounded by virgins)	Ursula
Basket of fruit & flowers	Dorothea/Dorothy
Basket or pitcher	Zita
Basket with loaves	Philip
Beehive	Ambrose; Bernard of Clairvaux; John Chrysostom
Beggar	Edith of Wilton (washing feet of beggar)
Beggar (receiving cloak)	Martin
Bell	Anthony Abbot
Bones	Ambrose
Book	many saints hold a gospel
Book	Virgin Mary in Annunciation & as Mary, Mother of all Wisdom
Book & crook	Chad
Books	Ambrose or Boniface
Bottle/pilgrim flask	James the Great
Box or vase	Mary Magdalene (with long hair)
Breasts, on plate	Agatha
Candle (devil blowing it out)	Genevieve

Capstan	Erasmus, Bishop of Formiae or Elmo
Cauldron of oil	Vitus
Chains	Leonard or Peter (in prison)
Child on arm	Anthony of Padua
Child Jesus on shoulder	Christopher (crossing river)
Child, crucified	William of Norwich
Children (male) carried (2)	Eustace
Children in tub (3)	Nicholas of Myra
Children, male (2)	Mary, wife of Cleophas
Church (model of)	Withburga (2 does at feet) or Botolph or other founder
Cloth (imprinted with face of Christ)	Veronica
Comb (iron)	Bishop Blaise
Cross (inverted)	Peter
Cross (red on white)	George
Cross (saltire)	Andrew
Crown of roses	Cecilia
Crown of roses or holding roses	Dorothy or Teresa
Demon at feet	Norbert (in white habit)
Devil trampled on by man in armour	Michael
Devil with bellows	Genevieve
Drug jars	Cosmas and Damian
Eyes on dish	Lucy
Flame in hand/breast	Anthony of Padua
Fuller's club	James the Less
Gridiron	Laurence or Vincent
Halberd	Jude
Head (own, carried before altar)	Winefride or Osyth
Head (own mitred & carried)	Bishop Denis
Head (of St Oswald crowned & carried)	Bishop Cuthbert
Head (man's under feet)	Catherine of Alexandria
Heart (flaming or transfixed by sword)	Augustine of Hippo

ATTRIBUTES AND ALLEGORY
Saints

Hermit	Anthony Abbot	Scythe & carrying head	Sidwell or Sithewell
Horseshoe	Bishop Eloi		
Idols (broken)	Wilfrid (baptising pagans)	Scythe & oxen (2)	Walstan
		Set-square	Thomas
Keys	Peter; Zita; Martha (at girdle)	Shears	Agatha
		Sieve (broken)	Benedict
Knife & skin over arm	Bartholomew	Staff	James the Great; James the Less; Bridget of Sweden or Anthony Abbot
Lily	Euphemia; Joseph; Dominic (in black & white habit); Catherine of Siena (usually in Dominican habit)	Stone (striking head)	Stephen
		Sword	Paul or Barbara
Loaves	Olaf & Zita	Sword through breast	Euphemia
Loaves & fishes	disciples		
Manacles	Leonard (holding them)	Sword through neck	Lucy
Medical equipment	Cosmas & Damian	T-shaped or Tau cross	Philip
Millstone	Vincent	T-shaped or Tau cross on shoulder	Anthony Abbot
Musical instruments	Cecilia		
Olive branch	Agnes	Together	Cosmas & Damian; Raphael & Tobias; (carrying fish); Peter & Paul; Philip & James
Pagans being baptised	Wilfrid		
Palm leaf	any martyr		
Peacock feather	Barbara	Tower	Barbara
Pen, ink & scroll	Mark; Matthew; Bernard of Clairvaux	Tree	Etheldreda (asleep)
		Tree (foot on fallen tree)	Bishop Boniface
Pincers	Agatha; Dunstan; Apollonia (holding tooth)	True Cross	Helen
		Weighing souls	Michael
Portrait of Virgin Mary	Luke	Wheel	Catherine of Alexandria (man's head under feet)
Roses in lap	Elizabeth of Hungary	Winged man	Matthew
Pot of holy water & aspergillum	Martha (or as housewife, with kitchen pot & ladle)	Wounded forehead (red band)	Bridget of Sweden
Saw	Simon	Wounded leg	Roch (also with angel, dog, staff or shell)
Scallop shell	James the Great		
Scourge	Ambrose	Wounds of Christ (*stigmata*)	Francis of Assisi

SAINTS AND APOSTLES

Apostles are marked ★, there are always 12, but not always the same saints. Jude, Simon and Matthias are not always included. Apostles may also carry scrolls which contain the creed. The principal attribute of each saint is highlighted and shown first.

Adrian	**anvil**; axe; sword
Agatha	**dish containing her breasts**; pincers; shears
Agnes	**lamb**; olive branch; palm
Aidan	**flaming torch**; stag at feet;
Alban	**sword**; fountain; his head in his hands; mace
Alphege	**chasuble full of stones**, or a battle axe
Ambrose	**beehive**; books; 2 human bones; scourge with 3 knots
★ Andrew	**saltire cross**
Anthony Abbot	**stick with T-shaped handle** or Tau cross on shoulder; bell; pig; fire
Anthony of Padua	**Franciscan habit**; infant Christ in arms; flame in hand or on breast; kneeling mules
Apollonia	**pincers holding tooth**
Augustine of Canterbury	**dressed as archbishop**
Augustine of Hippo	**flaming heart transfixed by two arrows**; dressed as bishop; books
Barbara	**tower**; cup and wafer; peacock's feather; cannon; crown
★ Barnabas	**Tudor roses on shield** or gospel
★ Bartholomew	**knife**; his skin held over his arm
Benedict	**Benedictine habit** (black, or white of the reformed order); broken cup; sprinkler; raven with loaf in beak; broken sieve
Bernard of Clairvaux	**white habit with pastoral staff**; beehive; inkhorn; pen; three mitres; bound dragon
Blaise	**iron comb**; dressed as bishop
Boniface	**book transfixed by sword** or stained with blood; foot on fallen tree; dressed as archbishop
Botolph	**dressed as abbot**
Bridget of Sweden	**taper or candle**; crozier; staff; red band across forehead
Catherine of Alexandria	**wheel**; head of man under feet; sword and book
Catherine of Siena	**cross with lily**; white tunic and veil with black cloak; book or rosary in hands
Cecilia	**musical instruments**; crown of roses
Chad	**St. Chad's cross**; book and crook
Christopher	**carrying infant Christ across river**
Clare	**pyx or monstrance**; dressed as nun; cross; lily
Clement	**anchor**; dressed as Pope or bishop
Cosmas & Damian	**medical equipment**; always together; dressed as physicians
Cuthbert	**St Oswald's crowned head in hands**; dressed as bishop; otter
David of Wales	**dove on shoulder**; dressed as bishop; bible
Denis	**dressed as bishop**; carries his own head

ATTRIBUTES & ALLEGORY
Saints

Dominic	**black and white dogs with torch in mouth**; star on forehead; lily; black and white habit
Dorothea/Dorothy	**basket of roses**; roses and apples; crown of roses
Dunstan	**gold cup on blue field**; red hot pincers
Edith of Wilton	**washing feet of beggar**
Edmund	**crowned and pierced by arrows**; dressed as king; wolf guarding head; arrow
Edward	**dressed as king**; sceptre surmounted by dove; ring
Elizabeth	**in Salutation scenes** and with her son, John the Baptist
Eloi or Eligius	**anvil**; dressed as bishop; hammer and tongs; horseshoe; bellows at feet
Erasmus	**capstan**; dressed as bishop; sailing ship
Etheldreda	**dressed as nun**; crowned; building church; asleep under tree
Euphemia	**sword through breast**; lion; bear; lily
Eustace	**stag with crucifix between horns**; carrying his two sons across river; brass bull
Francis of Assisi	**birds**; lamb; lily; stigmata
Frideswide	**dressed as abbess**, crowned; gospels
Genevieve	**crook or distaff**; dressed as nun; devil blowing out lighted candle relit by angel; sheep; basket of loaves
George	**red cross** on white ground on banner or breast; white horse; dragon
Giles	**hind pierced by arrow**; arrow piercing hand and stag
Gregory	**dressed as pope**; dove on shoulder; dove hovering overhead
Helena	**dressed as empress**; large cross (True cross)
Hubert	**dressed as hunter or bishop**; stag with crucifix between horns, beside him or crouched on book
Hugh of Lincoln	**swan**; Carthusian habit; three flowers
Ives or Yvo	**dressed as lawyer**; surrounded by widows and orphans
★ James the Great	**scallop shell**; staff; bottle; pilgrim's broad-brimmed hat
★ James the Less	**fuller's staff** or club
Jerome	**cardinal's hat**; **lion**; as man of learning at desk or in desert
Joachim	**meeting St Anne** at Golden Gate; basket with two doves
John Chrysostom	**dove at ear**; beehive; chalice; gospels
John de Matha	**white habit** with blue/red cross on breast; fetters; angels leading captives
John the Baptist	**hairy coat**; lamb; tall staff with cross piece;
★ John the Evangelist	**eagle**; cup with serpent
Joseph	**flowering rod**; doves in cage or basket
Joseph of Arimathaea	**shroud**; crown of thorns; nails
★ Jude	**halberd**; club; lance
Julian of le Mans	**blue cross-crosslet saltire wise on silver shield**
Juliana of Nicanedia	**devil flogged** or held in chains
Laurence	**gridiron**
Leonard	**broken fetters**; dressed as deacon or abbot; holding chains; manacles
Louis IX	**crown of thorns**; dressed as king or Franciscan; three nails of the cross
Lucy	**eyes in dish**; lamp; sword; wound in neck

★ Luke the Evangelist	**winged ox**; painting a portrait of Virgin Mary
Margaret of Antioch	**rising from belly of dragon**; dragon; palm; cross
★ Mark the Evangelist	**winged lion**; pen; ink; scroll
Martha	**leading dragon**; aspergillum; ladle; keys at girdle;
Martin	**giving half cloak to beggar**; dressed as bishop; goose at feet
Mary, dau of Cleophas	**four sons** (James the Less, Jude, Simon, Joseph) and their attributes
Mary, wife of Zebedee	**two sons** (John the Evangelist, James the Great) and their attributes
Mary Magdalene	**vase or box** of ointment; long blonde hair; or as Penitent Harlot, barely clothed usually holding a crucifix and with a skull beside her, sometimes her cast-off jewellery at her feet
★ Matthew the Evangelist	**winged man**; ink; scroll; pen; bag of money; knife; dagger
★ Matthias	**axe**; halberd
Nicholas of Myra	**three golden balls or purses**; dressed as bishop; ship; anchor; three children in tub
Norbert	**dressed in white habit** over black; devil bound at feet; spider in chalice; monstrance or ciborium
Olaf	**loaves**
Oswald	**dressed as king**; sceptre; cross; silver dish
Osyth or Sytha	**dressed as queen** or abbess; own head in hands
★ Paul	**sword**; beard
★ Peter	**keys**; fish; inverted cross; beard; curly hair
Peter the Martyr	**dressed as Dominican**; wound in head
★ Philip	**cross**; T-shaped cross; basket of loaves
Radegunda	**dressed as abbess** (crowned); kneeling captive at feet; holding broken fetters
Roch	**pointing at plague sore on leg**; dog; staff; shell; angel
Sebastian	**bound to tree** or column; pierced by arrows
Sidwell or Sithewell	**scythe**; well; head in hands
★ Simon	**saw**; fishes; cross
Stephen	**stone striking head**; dressed as deacon
Swithin	**dressed as bishop** (Winchester)
Sylvester	**bound**; dressed as pope; two dead pagans; spear; dagger
Teresa of Avila	**dressed in brown habit**; roses; dragon
★ Thomas	**builder's set-square**; ruler; girdle; spear or lance
Thomas à Becket	**dressed as archbishop** or Benedictine; wound in head
Thomas Aquinas	**dressed as Dominican**; star on breast
Ursula	**arrow in hand** or pierced by one; surrounded by handmaidens; banner (red cross on white)
Veronica	**cloth marked with head of Christ** (vernicle)
Vincent	dressed as deacon; raven; gridiron; millstone; whip in hand

Saints

Vitus	**cauldron of oil**; boy with palm; cock; lion; wolf
Walstan	**crowned**; scythe in hand; two oxen at feet
Wilfrid	**baptising pagans**; broken idols
William of Norwich	**child crucified**; cross and nails; hammer and nails
Winefred	**own head** in hands before altar; sword; palm branch; book
Withburga	**two does at feet**; church in hand
Wulfstan, Wulstan or Wolstan	**dressed as bishop**; fixing crozier in tomb (of St Edmund) devil with book; giving sight to blind man
Zita, Citha or Sitha	**as housekeeper**; keys; loaves; rosary; bag; pitcher; basket

EVANGELISTS

As saints, the four gospel writers may have several attributes, but where they are given prominence as evangelists one only is usual.

Matthew	Mark	Luke	John
winged man	winged lion	winged ox	eagle

ANGELIC ORDERS

Archangels

Gabriel	the messenger of God (therefore in scenes of the Annunciation)
Michael	chief archangel; weighs souls; expulsion of Adam and Eve from Eden; killing a dragon
Raphael	the Guardian Angel, shown with Tobias and his fish
Uriel	most obscure of the Archangels, sometimes known as the Regent of the Sun, shown holding the sun; carries a book or scroll; almost never shown without the other three archangels
Angels	one pair of wings; halo; holding scrolls, instruments of the Passion or musical instruments
Cherubim	depicted with heads only and six wings; wings may be strewn with eyes; may be depicted as warriors or judges; conventionally painted blue
Seraphim	as Cherubim but painted red
Thrones	scarlet wheels with wings, sometimes strewn with eyes
Prophets	Amos, Daniel, Ezekiel, Habakkuk, Haggai, Hosea, Isaiah, Jeremiah, Joel, Jonah, Malachi, Micah, Nahum, Obadiah, Zechariah, Zephaniah

LATIN DOCTORS
The medieval church recognised four principal scholars of the church

Augustine	dressed as bishop or doctor
Ambrose	dressed as bishop
Gregory	dressed as pope
Jerome	dressed as cardinal

HOLY ORDERS
Each of the Holy Orders has its own characteristic dress or habit. Saints who were also monks or prelates are often depicted wearing the dress of their order and/or rank.

Benedictine	black habit *Benedict; Boniface; Thomas à Becket*
Carmelite	white cloak over brown habit (since 1297) *John de Matha, with blue/red cross on breast, fetters or angel leading captives*
Carthusian	white habit *Hugh of Lincoln, with swan and three flowers*
Cistercian	white or grey habit *Bernard of Clairvaux, with three crowns*
Dominican	white tunic, black cloak with hood (monks and nuns) *Dominic, with star on forehead and two dogs carrying torches; Peter the Martyr, with wound in head; Thomas Aquinas, with chalice and star on breast*
Franciscan	brown or grey habit *Francis of Assisi, with birds or animals; Anthony of Padua, with infant Christ; Louis IX, with crown of thorns*
Knights Templar	white wool habit with red cross
Knights of St John	long full black tunic with white cross on breast (red surcoat for high ranks)
Martyrs	palm frond
Hermits	T-shaped staff; rosary
Pilgrims	hat with shell; staff; wallet
Founders	model of church or monastery in hand
Abbots and Bishops	pastoral staff or crozier
Archbishops	dressed in pall *Boniface; Augustine of Canterbury; Thomas à Becket*
Popes	triple tiara; cope; pallium; triple cross in hand
Cardinals	red hat; red cloak; red robe *Jerome*

KINGS
Kings and Queens are usually richly dressed and crowned
Kings
Edmund; Edward the Confessor; Oswald; Louis IX
Queens
Helen; Frideswide; Elizabeth of Hungary, Margaret of Scotland
Emperor
holding imperial standard or labarum (see page 28) bearing cross and Chi Rho symbol *Constantine the Great*

BIBLICAL SCENES

Certain scenes, stories and themes from the Bible are often represented, sometimes with titles. There are many variations, but some of the most common scenes described in a series of respresentations are indicated here.

Types and Antitypes

Types *(Old Testament incidents)* are often balanced by or used to foreshadow **antitypes** *(New Testament incidents)* in Christian decoration. Jonah was trapped in the whale for three days, for example, the same period of time as Christ's entombment, and the two scenes often appear together to symbolise the Resurrection. The scenes in the windows of King's College Chapel, Cambridge are a type/antitype scheme.

NEW TESTAMENT
The Passion Cycle

Entry into Jerusalem; Last Supper; Washing of the Disciples' feet; Agony in the Garden; Betrayal; Denial of Peter; Trial of Christ; Mocking of Christ; Flagellation; Crowning with Thorns; Ecce Homo; Stations of the Cross; Road to Calvary; Christ stripped of his Garments; Raising of the Cross; Crucifixion *(Virgin Mary and John or Virgin Mary and soldier, Longinus, with lance to Christ's right, John and Stephaton, with reed and sponge, to His left);* Descent from the Cross; Pieta *(Virgin Mary supporting dead Christ);* Joseph of Arimathea removing nails and taking Body for burial; Entombment; Resurrection; three Maries at the Tomb; Mary Magdalene encountering Christ at Tomb *(noli me tangere);* Journey to Emmaus; Supper at Emmaus (with two disciples); Incredulity of Thomas; Ascension; Descent of the Holy Ghost.

The Stations of the Cross

Jesus condemned to death; Jesus receives the Cross; Jesus falls under the Cross; Jesus meets the Virgin Mary; Simon of Cyrene bears the Cross; Veronica wipes the face of Jesus; Jesus falls for the second time; Jesus meets the women of Jerusalem; Jesus falls for the third time; Jesus is stripped of His garments; Jesus is nailed to the Cross; Jesus dies on the Cross; Jesus is taken down from the Cross; The body of Jesus is laid in the sepulchre.

The Life of the Virgin

Joachim and Anne, *(parents of the Virgin);* Nativity; Presentation in the Temple; Marriage; Annunciation; Visitation *(meeting of Mary and Elizabeth);* Death; Assumption; Coronation.
The Virgin also appears in other scenes:
Nativity; Adoration of the Shepherds; Adoration of the Magi; Circumcision of Christ; Presentation in the Temple *(prophecy of Simeon);* Flight into Egypt; Descent from the Cross; Portrait being painted by St. Luke.

Miracles and Parables

Marriage at Cana *(changing water into wine);* Feeding of the 4000 *(with seven loaves and a few fishes);* Feeding of the 5000 *(with five loaves and two fishes);* Raising of Lazarus from the Dead; Miraculous Draught of Fishes; Sermon on the Mount *(The Beatitudes);* Return of the Prodigal Son; The Good Shepherd; The Good Samaritan; and so on.

OLD TESTAMENT
The Creation; Adam and Eve; Noah building the Ark; The Flood; The Sacrifice of Isaac; Moses and the Burning Bush; Samson killing a lion or the Philistine; Moses striking the Rock; Moses and the Brazen Serpent; Joshua and the Walls of Jericho; Jonah and the Whale; Jacob's Ladder; Joseph and the Coat of Many Colours; David and Goliath; The Judgement of Solomon; Solomon and the Queen of Sheba; Ruth gleaning the corn; etc. etc.

APOCRYPHA
Tobias and the Angel; Judith and Holofernes; Susanna and the Elders.

TEXTS
The same biblical texts were repeatedly used in inscriptions and wall paintings. Their usual sources are the King James Authorised Version of the Bible, the Latin Bible (Vulgate), the Book of Common Prayer or the Roman Catholic Missal.

Ave Maria, Creed, Sanctus	Book of Common Prayer
The Beatitudes	Matthew 5: 3-10
The Fruits of the Spirit	Paul's Letter to the Galatians 5
The Gifts of the Holy Spirit	Isaiah 11: 1-2
The Magnificat	Luke 1: 46-55
Words from the Cross	Luke 23: 34, 43, 46; John 19: 26-28, 30; Matthew 27: 46

ALLEGORICAL SYMBOLS FROM THE OLD TESTAMENT

Altar of sacrifice or burnt offering	Old Testament worship
Apple	Fall of Man
Ark of the Covenant	presence of God
Bullock and censer	Day of Atonement
Butterflies	escape of soul to afterlife
Caterpillars	man's earthly life
Distaff	destiny of Eve
Doorposts and lintel	God's protection at Passover
Dove with olive branch	peace and forgiveness
Dragon	Satan; sin; pestilence
Dragon (underfoot)	victory of good over evil
Flaming sword held by angel or Hand of God	expulsion of Adam from Eden
Grapes	entry into Canaan
Lamb (paschal lamb)	Feast of Passover
Lash & bricks	captivity of Israel
Lizards, beetles, snails	transience of life and decay of the body
Scroll	Torah or five books of Moses
Scroll & sheaf of wheat	Pentecost
Serpent	Satan
Serpent coiled around world	sinful nature of mankind
Serpent eating tail	serpent of eternity
Seven-branch candlestick (Menorah)	Old Testament worship
Spade	destiny of Adam

ATTRIBUTES & ALLEGORY
The Bible

Characters' attributes

Aaron	censer; flowering wand or rod in hand
Abel	crook; lamb
Abraham	knife; shield
Amos	crook
Cain	plough
Daniel	ram with four horns
David	harp; lion
Deborah	crown
Elijah	fiery chariot; wheel of chariot; ravens
Esau	bow and arrows
Ezekiel	closed gate
Gideon	pitcher concealing torch
Hosea	cast-off mantle
Isaac	cross formed of bundles of wood
Isaiah	saw; book; scroll
Jacob and family	sun, moon and twelve stars
Jeremiah	large stone
Jonah	whale
Joseph	coat of many colours
Joshua	trumpet; sword
Melchisedek	loaf and chalice
Micah	temple on mountain
Moses	bullrush basket; burning bush; horns; tablets
Nahum	feet appearing from cloud above mountain
Noah	ark; oar; dove with olive branch
Ruth	ear of wheat
Samson	jawbone of ass; pillars; wrestling with lion; head in lap of Delilah
Seth	thread wound three times around thumb
Solomon	temple (model of)
Zephaniah	sword over Jerusalem

Magi

Caspar	old man with long beard (often represents Europe)
Melchoir	middle aged man with short beard (often represents Asia)
Balthazar	young man; shown as a negro (for Africa) when the Magi represent the three continents

Early decorators of churches used a whole series of symbols which had specific meanings for worshippers and clergy. Symbols can be confusing and need to be read in the right context. An eagle, for example, apart from being an attribute of St John the Evangelist, can also signify magnanimity or the Resurrection, and secularly the sense of Sight.

Power or blessing (Latin form)

Power or blessing (Greek form)

With Souls of the Righteous

Judgement

Blessing   Judgement

Pre-9th century attitude of prayer

Argument

Nimbus worn by dead saint or biblical person

Speech   Condemnation

Nimbus worn by living person when portrayed

Supplication

Mandorla or Vesica piscis *(almond shaped frame which encloses the entire body of Christ or the BVM)*

ATTRIBUTES & ALLEGORY
Symbols

Stars

Seven Gifts of the Spirit (see page 29)

Nine Fruits of the Spirit

Twelve tribes of Israel

Regeneration

Creator

Epiphany

Sacred Monograms

Chi Rho
(the first two letters of the Greek word for Christ XPICTOC)

IHC or IHS
(the first letters of the Greek spelling of Jesus IHOCYC)

Jesus Christ Victor
N = nika (victor) or nostra (our)

Alpha and Omega
first and last letters of the Greek alphabet
(Beginning and End of all things)

Chi Rho with Alpha and Omega in a circle
(symbol of Christ within symbol for eternity)

Alpha Mu Omega
yesterday, today and evermore

The Cornerstone

24

SYMBOLS OF THE HOLY TRINITY

Trefoil

Triquetra

Interlocking Traingles

Circle within Triangle

Interwoven Circles

Triquetra and Circle

Holy Trinity

Trinity Star or Star of David

Equilateral Triangle

The Three Fishes

The Three Hares

Shield with Doctrine of the Blessed Trinity

Triangle in Circle

Cruciform or three-rayed nimbus worn by the Trinity

ATTRIBUTES & ALLEGORY
Symbols

SYMBOLS OF THE PASSION CYCLE

 Crown of Thorns

 Sponge on Reed

 Nails

 Thirty Pieces of Silver

 Scourges

 Hammer and Pincers

 Dice and Seamless Robe

 The Cock that Crowed

 Cross with shroud or winding sheet

 Pillar and Cords

 The Title from Iesus Nazarene Rex Iudacorum *(Jesus of Nazareth, King of the Jews)*

 Fist that buffeted Him

 Lantern

 Jug of Vinegar

 Five Wounds

 Agony in Gethsemane

 Ladder

 Sword and Staff

ATTRIBUTES & ALLEGORY

Seven Lamps or Seven Flames

Seven Doves

The Holy Spirit
The Dove

Agnus Dei with
Book of Seven Seals

Agnus Dei with
Banner of Victory

The Pelican in her Piety
(the pelican piercing its breast to feed its young with its blood is a symbol of Christ's sacrifice on the cross)

The Greek word for fish signifies
Jesus Christ Son of God, Saviour

Paschal Lamb
Old Testament

ATTRIBUTES & ALLEGORY
Symbols

ATTRIBUTES & ALLEGORY

SYMBOLS OF THE BLESSED VIRGIN MARY (BVM)

Mater Dei

Rose without a Thorn

Crescent moon

Lily

Pierced heart

Snowdrop

Winged heart

SYMBOLS OF POWER

Temporal figures may carry a staff of office or a specific symbol signifying power and authority. Archibishops, bishops and abbots may carry a crozier, pastoral staff or a Primatial staff. The pastoral staff will be carried in the right hand except during benediction when it will be in the left hand. On the eve of battle in 312AD Constantine saw in a dream a cross in the sky, and heard a voice saying 'In hoc signo vinces,' *(By this sign shalt thou conquer).* It is said after that he substituted the Chi Rho emblem for the Roman eagle on the standard, or **labarum**, of the legions.

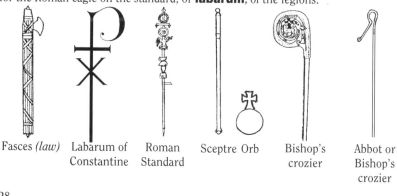

Fasces *(law)*

Labarum of Constantine

Roman Standard

Sceptre

Orb

Bishop's crozier

Abbot or Bishop's crozier

GROUPS OF SEVEN
Seven is the symbolic number of perfection

Gifts of the Holy Spirit
Wisdom
Understanding
Counsel
Fortitude
Knowledge
True Godliness/Piety
Fear of the Lord

Liberal Arts
(sometimes accompanied by virtues)
Arithmetic
Astronomy
Geometry
Grammar
Logic
Music
Rhetoric

Sacraments
Baptism
Confirmation
Communion (Eucharist)
Penance (Confession)
Holy Orders
Matrimony
Extreme Unction

Vices or Deadly Sins
Anger
Covetousness
Envy
Gluttony
Lust
Pride
Sloth

Virtues (generally female)

Faith	**holding a cross**; chalice; foot resting on a square stone block
Hope	**holding an anchor**; eyes and hands raised to Heaven; sometimes with wings
Charity	**nursing a child**; surrounded by children or holding vase with flames; holding a flaming heart
Justice	**scales**; sword; blindfold
Prudence	**holding a snake and mirror**; sometimes with two faces looking in both directions simultaneously, sometimes the snake is a dragon
Temperance	**pouring liquid from one vessel to another** (watering the wine); sheathed sword; two vases
Fortitude	**dressed in armour resembling Minerva**; sword; club; shield; broken pillar; lion

COSTUME
Biblical

100BC-100AD

Depictions in medieval or later churches may be based upon fairly accurate knowledge of what was worn in a specific area or date or may, especially in late coloured glass window lights, be the invention of the artist.

The illustrations on pages 30 and 31 show the type of garments worn in the century before the birth of Christ and up to 200AD. Although we do not possess actual items of dress, with the exception of leather and metal footwear, belts and armour and the Bronze Age woollen garments preserved in Danish peat bogs, our knowledge of what was worn is fairly accurate. It comes from the written word, Tactics for example, from sculpture, metal and stone relief-work and from wall and tomb paintings. These drawings are an accurate depiction from these sources.

Garments worn in this period were not fitted to the figure, such skill only developed during the Middle Ages. The amount of seam sewing and the fabric and decoration used varied according to the area; this was affected by climate, religion and local custom. For example, Hebrew garments, though loose, shapeless and worn in layers, were sewn at the sides and shoulders and had sleeves. Persian dress was also sewn. We owe the introduction of the coat to the Persians. The classical dress of Greece and Rome, in contrast, was draped, largely unsewn and held to the body by belts and brooches. It consisted of rectangles of fabric for tunics, gowns and cloaks.

1 Persian dress wearing long coat over belted tunic, trousers and shoes. Curled beard and hair. 2 Hebrew dress. Tunics(kethoneth) with shawl (tallith) on top. The tassels (tsitsith) have religious significance

3 Persian shoe
4 Roman sandal

7 Greek hairstyle
8 Roman hairstyle

5 Persian linen headdress

12, 13 Roman draped dress 1st century AD. The man wears leather, laced boots

9, 10 Greek draped costume 1st century BC. Fastened to figure by girdles and shoulder brooches

6 Hebrew turban

11 Roman lady's coiffure

Drawings by Doreen Yarwood *Encyclopaedia of World Costume* Batsford

1ST TWO CENTURIES AD

1-2 British   3-5 Franks and Gauls

The dress shown on this page reflects that worn in Europe at this time. We have detailed understanding of such attire, partly from written records, accounts such as *The Agricola* and *The Germania* written AD98 by the Roman historian Cornelius Tacitus, also from sculptured reliefs, notable those on the columns of Trajan (AD114) and Marcus Aurelius (AD174) in Rome. A life-size replica of the former is on display in the Victoria and Albert Museum in London. Apart from Spain, the colder climate of much of Europe compared with the Middle East, necessitated wearing warmer clothes. In the climate of Greece and Rome fine linens, pleated fabrics and imported silks were available and styles were sophisticated (page 30). In northern Europe the chief textile was wool with fur linings. Garments were loose but sewn, Shoes, if worn, were of untanned hide. Legs were bare or trousered. These latter were loose and shapeless, tied at waist and ankle with drawstring.

6-7 Spain 8-10 Teutonic tribesman

Drawings by Doreen Yarwood *European Costume* Batsford

COSTUME
Early Middle Ages up to 1340

2 Surcoat & coif 1245

4 Surcoat, hood, liripipe 1310

5 Hood, liripipe 1340

1 Tabard c1200

3 Gardecorps 1270

Throughout this period garments were still loose and ill-fitting, sew only down the side seams. Men wore ankle-or knee-length tunics, women gowns, both were cut similarly. Back and front of the garment were cut in one piece with a round hole made for the head. There were thus no shoulder seams or set-in sleeves, the sleeves being cut in one with the garment leaving wide armholes. Fabrics were chiefly wool and linen though, as a result of the Crusades, increased trade brought importation of richer fabrics from Italy and the East for the wealthy. 13th century dress was noted for its extreme simplicity of line and lack of decoration. During this century the **surcoat** (surcote) was introduced. It began as a tabard, a simple, unsewn garment originating as a covering for the armour of the Crusading knight in order to conceal the sun's glare on the metal. The tabard slowly developed into the longer, sleeveless surcoat worn by both sexes. Later, long, open sleeves were introduced (**gardecorps**). Underwear, (both sexes) comprised a long linen shirt or chemise and knee-length long shapeless underpants held by a drawstring at the waist (**braies**). These were tucked into cloth stockings and gartered. Men wore a linen cap (**coif**) and, on top, a hat or, more commonly, a hood with shoulder cape. After 1300 the point on top lengthened into a long tail (**liripipe**). Women's long hair was plaited in coils and encased in a net. This could be accompanied by a draped gorget (**wimple**) and/or chin band (**barbette**) and cap, all in white linen.

6 Gown, mantle 1320

10 Net, barbette, cap 1260

11 Wimple, (gorget) c1300

7 Surcoat 1265

9 Leather boot

12 Net (crispine) 1240

8 Veil, barbette 1200

Drawings by Doreen Yarwood English Costume Batsford

1 Fur-trimmed velvet sideless surcoat 1360

2 Parti-coloured tunic & hose 1350

3 1365

4 Houppelande 1415

5 Chaperon 1455

After 1340 dress changed radically. Man had learned to tailor and clothes cut and sewn to fit the figure were made. Both masculine tunic and feminine gown were cut in four sections and seamed at front, back and sides. Sleeves were inset. Men's tunics of 1350 were hip-length with a hip belt. Gradually they became shorter and shorter. To complement this, hose became longer and braies shorter. Hose then became tights with a bag at the fork (**codpiece**). They were of fabric, not knitted and were seamed in four sections. The tunic and gowns were waisted (**cotehardie**). Ladies wore a full surcoat on top. Then, suited to the older and less slender, came the loose houppelande worn by both sexes. Decoration became rich and varied: parti-colouring; dagged edges; fur trimming. Fabrics became richer: velvets; satins; brocade. The masculine hood became a padded roll with liripipe (**chaperon**). Tall hats were fashionable. Ladies' headdresses took many elaborate forms: wired cauls; heart-shaped designs; horned shapes. Veils accompanied most headdresses. Hair was completely hidden.

6 Padded long tunic 1450

7 Houppelande 1435

8 Houppelande 1445

9 Young man of fashion 1450

Drawings by Doreen Yarwood *European Costume* Batsford

COSTUME

COSTUME
Spread of the Renaissance 1465-1540

1 Gown 1475

2 Gable hood 1500

3 1520

4 c1495

5 Fashionable youth 1505

Costume, no less than the other arts of mankind, reflects current events and important movements. The Renaissance, which had begun much earlier in Italy, by this time had brought its cult of Humanism to northern Europe. The effects could be seen in close-fitting male garments intended to display the human figure; this was evidenced especially in the hose, very short tunics, long hair and swashbuckling hats (5). Young men, in particular, followed such fashions, older men were more discreet (1). The Reformation began to show its effect on dress in the early 16th century in a greater covering up of the figure and use of heavier materials (9). For ladies, the Spanish **farthingale** made its appearance. This was a canvas underskirt reinforced by circular whalebone hoops extending from waist to ground. It was accompanied by strict corseting to provide a slender waist and uplifted breasts (6). A variety of feminine hoods developed from the late 15th century steeple headdress (7, 8, 10).

6 Farthingale gown 1535

8 Gable hood 1515

9 1530

10 Gable hood 1536

7 Steeple headdress 1470

11 1515

12 Velvet shoe

Drawings by Doreen Yarwood *European Costume* Batsford

34

1 Farthingale,
French hood
c1547

2 Princess Mary
c1545

3 Ruff, doublet,
trunk hose 1580

4 Queen Elizabeth
c1590

Fashion in dress has always been set and practised by the wealthy, important section of society. In a wider context it has been the nations which, at any given time, were the most powerful which initiated the mode. In the years 1540-1620 the dominant country was Spain. From here came the **cape**, the **doublet**, the **trunk hose** and the **ruff**, the **corset** and **farthingale**. Never before or since, has fashionable dress been so rich, so be-jewelled and embroidered. It was overseas exploration and the discovery of the New World which brought these riches and influence. Not only was the costume richly decorative but the fashion was to mould the human figure to an artificial form by bombast and restriction. Men wore corsets and padded their doublets and trunk hose; women wore ever-wider farthingales and tighter corsets. Both sexes displayed starched and supported cartwheel ruffs. Relaxation only began to appear from about 1610.

COSTUME

5 Making music 1611
Spinet and lute
More natural, less
restrictive garments

Drawings by Doreen Yarwood *Fashion of the Western World* Batsford

COSTUME
Elegance and naturalism 1620-1660

1 Dashing cavalier 1630-5

2 Mrs Tradescant Puritan hat and cap 1645

3 Charles I 1638-40

4 Queen Henrietta Maria 1635-40

5 Prince Charles c1636

By 1620 the pendulum of fashion had swung sharply away from restriction and bombast. Spanish influence waned and the centre of importance had moved to the Low Countries which continued to be the dominant factor until France, under Louis XIV, began its long reign over fashion in the 1660s. Professor Randolph Schwabe, late Director of the Slade College of Art, once described the dress of the years 1620-60 as 'long locks, lace and leather'. With reference to masculine dress this was particularly apt. It was an age of elegance, long hair (natural, not a wig) plumed Cavalier hats, a large lace collar to replace the ruff, jacket and breeches and those superbly soft leather boots, their open buckets tops frothing with lace boot hose. Ladies' dress was less impressive but on similar lines: corset and farthingale had gone. In England the Puritan version of the style was basically the same theme but stripped of all decoration and lace, a tall black hat replacing the plumed one.

6-12 Portrait of a Flemish family c1655-60. Children dressed as miniatures of their parents

Drawings by Doreen Yarwood *European Costume* Batsford

1 William III Periwig 1700

3 Lady's shoe

2 Queen Mary 1694

4 Gentleman's shoe

5 & 6 1665

Men's dress in the 1660s (6) continued to be elegant and comfortable. The jacket became much shorter to display a full white shirt finished at the neck with a lace-edged cravat. This was the era of petticoat breeches (correctly termed **rhinegraves** after the Count of that name who popularised them). They were very full, long shorts decorated by rows of ribbon loops. Hair was still long and flowing. Later in the 1660s came the introduction of the open coat (9). This garment originated in Persia (page 30 (1)). By 1680 the coat had become waisted and buttoned. It had large cuffs, but no collar due to the wig covering, and frogged decoration (7). Before the end of the century the multi-curled periwig had supplanted natural flowing hair (1, 7, 9). By this time ladies' dress had begun its slow return to corsetry to achieve a slender waist but, as yet, no framework petticoats. Tall wired lace headdresses echoed the male piled-up periwig curls (2).

7 Gentleman 1695

8 Lady with parasol 1689

9 Early style of coat 1665

COSTUME
France: Arbiter of Fashion 1715-1760

1 English gentleman 1735-45

2 Pig-tail wig 1740

3 Tie wig c1730

4 Black tricorne hat 1750

5 Lavender taffeta gown 1755-60

In these years France's dominant role was undisputed. In all the trades and skills essential to *la mode* she had built up total pre-eminence from dressmaking to haberdashery, textiles to corsetry. The French language was that of Europe's ruling class. In men's dress the three-piece suit (forerunner of that of the 1930s) - coat, waistcoat and breeches - was now established.

Coat and breeches were often of matching fabric and decoration; in contrast, the waistcoat would be richly embroidered or brocaded all over (1, 9). The now much smaller wig was powdered white with rice or wheatmeal with unfortunate livestock accompaniment. It was surmounted by the hat of the age: the **tricorne**. For ladies the framework petticoat was back, this time in hoop design or, as the French called it, **le panier** *(basket)*. In designs of the 1720s and 1730s the gown was loose-fitting, the rear falling in box pleats to ground level. By the 1750s the tightly-corseted waist was again marked, the gown elaborately decorated with ruffles and bows.

6 Portrait young girl 1715

7 & 8 Painting by de Troy of French dress 1728-31

9 Actual garments Paris 1738

Drawings by Doreen Yarwood *European Costume* Batsford

COSTUME

38

1 Actual dress 1799

2 Actual dress 1795

3 Portrait 1790

4 Hoop skirt 1770

5 Actual costume 1775

Styles of dress under French influence, especially for women, became more and more artificial in shape, less and less comfortable as the 18th century progressed. Corsets were tight, hooped skirts wide (4), gowns overdecorated and, most artificial of all, women adapted tall wigs as men had done nearly a century earlier but these were powdered and, often, ridiculously overdecorated (7, 8). Meanwhile, in England, simpler, more elegant styles of dress were evolving for both sexes and this **mode a l'anglaise**, as it was called, began to influence all of Europe except France. It is typified in portraits by Gainsborough and his colleagues (6-9). With the French Revolution came ideas of democracy and the origins in ancient Greece. Draped long skirts, thin fabrics, décolleté necklines and high waistlines replaced artificiality.

6-9 Actual costumes 1789-90

6

7

8

9

COSTUME

Red cap
White undercap

Long beard and hair

White cloak with
Red Cross on
shoulder

Staff with metal
shield showing a
Red Cross on a
white ground

Knight Templar
13th century

Flat helm

White
surcoat
with red
cross on
breast

Crusader
13th century

Morion helmet

Sleeveless jerkin

Doublet

Sash worn over cuirass

Swordbelt
Breeches
Hose

Musket

Thighboots

Soldier c1590

COSTUME

Knights in armour are found on tombs and memorial brasses and individual pieces of armour may be depicted on all manner of decoration. Genuine armour and firearms were stored in churches and some may still be found over tombs, although often mixed up and put on the wrong tombs over centuries.
(*See MONUMENTS: Brasses*)

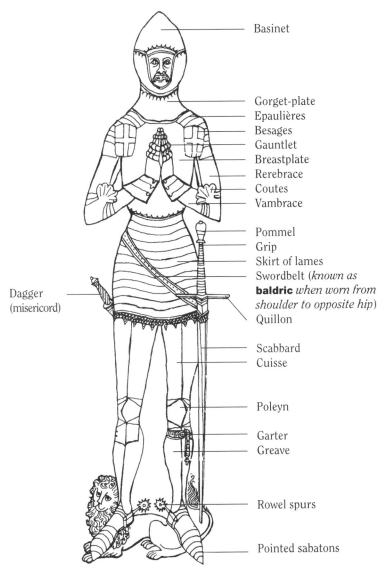

Basinet

Gorget-plate
Epaulières
Besages
Gauntlet
Breastplate
Rerebrace
Coutes
Vambrace

Pommel
Grip
Skirt of lames
Swordbelt (*known as* **baldric** *when worn from shoulder to opposite hip*)
Quillon

Dagger
(misericord)

Scabbard
Cuisse

Poleyn

Garter
Greave

Rowel spurs

Pointed sabatons

Knight 15th century

Lance with pennon

Boar spear

English bill

Partisan

Halberd

War hammer

Pollaxe

Roundel dagger

Falchion

Ballock dagger

Pommel

Scabbard

Grip

Crossbow

Quillon

Blade

Maces

Sword

Longbow

HELMETS

Flat-topped
Great Helm
1240-1300

Cap of Steel
1300-1450

Basinet
14th and early
15th century

Visored Sallet
late 15th century

Morion
1570-1600

Pikeman's Pot
17th century

**Funeral
helmet**
put together by
an undertaker
or herald
incorporating
bits of genuine
armour

Burgonet 16th
and 17th centuries

Mail coif

Hauberk

Mufflers

Sleeve of
hauberk

Surcoat

Swordbelt

Poleyns

Chausses

Basinet

Aventail

Jupon

Hip-belt

Tabard

**Early 14th century
knight**

14th century knight

16th century knight

COSTUME

Vestments

Alb	full length belted white tunic with narrow sleeves. Nowadays it is impossible to distinguish Anglican from Roman Catholic albs Sometimes embroidered at hem or trimmed with lace flounce and cuffs
Almuce	cape or scarf with hood, sometimes made of fur, or fur lined
Amice	white linen neck-cloth sometimes with an apparel at one edge
Apparel	decorated panel applied to albs and amices. Not found on 20th century albs but may be seen on early ones in stained glass, and brasses. Although seen with dalmatics, apparels are not fixed to dalmatics and are only fixed to the centre top of amices and, many years ago, to alb cuffs and hems front and back
Biretta	black, purple, red or white ridged hat, worn according to rank by priest, bishop, cardinal or pope
Cassock	full length sleeved gown, single or double breasted, black or coloured according to rank
Chasuble	circular or oval cape with central head opening and orphreys; the principal vestment worn by an officiating priest. Full tent-like chasuble often known as **romanesque**
Chimere	long sleeveless gown worn over the rochet
Clavi	decorative woven or embroidered bands found on early tunics and dalmatics
Cope	semicircular cape fastened with a **morse**, decorated with a hood and orphreys. 20th century copes are often hand-worked in combinations of kid-leather, beads, jewels, metallic threads, cords and stitchery, incorporating a variety of symbols (see page 156 for sample description)
Dalmatic	sleeved open-sided tunic, worn by deacons, decorated with stripes called clavi and sometimes with apparels
Girdle	white or coloured cord belt with tassels
Hood (academic)	worn by graduates in colours according to type of University degree
Hood (cope)	flat vestigial hood attached at back of cope
Lappets	pair of ribands *(ribbons)* attached at back of mitre
Maniple	decorated band worn over the left arm, resembling a short stole, originally a towel
Mitre	peaked headdress worn by bishops, popes and abbots: simplex = white; aurifrigiata = gold or silver on white; pretiosa = jewelled
Morse	clasp or fastening on the cope, often made of precious metals, enamelled and set with jewels. Can also be an embroidered band Originally metal only worn by a Bishop, fabric for others
Mozetta	short hooded cape, buttoned down front, coloured as rank
Orphrey	embroidered band, usually applied, found on chasubles and copes. On altar frontals, orphreys are decorative panels, loose or attached
Pallium	originally a woollen vestment worn by archbishops, usually shown as a narrow Y-shaped strip with embroidered crosses, falling down the centre front and back, now called 'Y' orphrey

COSTUME

Pastoral staff or Crozier	stave carried by high dignitaries on which may be a cross, crook or horizontal crook (**Tau stave**); sometimes a **vexillium** *(scarf)* is attached
Rochet	similar to alb but shorter, either sleeveless or sleeves gathered at wrist
Stole	decorated band worn round the neck, beneath the chasuble, resembling, but longer than, the maniple, usually with a device at each end and a cross at the neck
Surplice	white gown, differing from the alb by long flowing sleeves, worn unbelted over the cassock
Tiara	headdress of a pope
Tunicle	similar to dalmatic, although longer when worn by bishops with a dalmatic; it has narrow sleeves and no apparels except occasionally near the neck; it is usually worn by sub-deacons

Mitre
Primatial Cross

Apparel of
the amice

Pallium*

Maniple

Chasuble

Dalmatic
Tunicle

Stole

Apparel of
the alb
Buckskins

Archbishop
Medieval

*Pallium, forerunner
of the 'Y' orphrey

Bishop Andrews
cap

Ruff

Bishop sleeves
on Rochet

Chimere

Preaching scarf
Rochet

Archbishop
17th century

COSTUME

45

COSTUME
Vestments

Scarlet skull cap

White collar

Scarlet cloak with white lined shoulder cape (mozetta)

Scarlet biretta

White rochet

Scarlet cassock

Cardinal

Tonsure

Apparel of the amice

Romanesque style chasuble

Alb

Maniple

Stole

Apparel of the alb

Priest

DALMATICS

Tassels

Clavi

Traditional Dalmatic
with tassels and clavi

Dalmatic with clavi
20th century

COSTUME

GOTHIC CHASUBLES
with orphreys

Y-shaped

V-shaped

Pallium-shaped

Appliqued with Chi-Rho,
Alpha and Omega,
and cross motifs

Pillar shaped

COPES

Morse

Girdle

Orphrey

Alb

Orphrey of
the cope

Shield
shaped hood
with applied
Sacred
Monogram
and tassel

Cope

Alb

Cope with rounded and fringed hood with hand-embroidered Maltese cross and orphreys of coloured velvet

Lent/Advent cope with embroidered Crown of Thorns, Eclipse of the Sun and Star of Advent motifs

Cowl hood

Deacons' stoles	worn from the left shoulder to right hip
Organists' cassocks and surplices	usually with fuller skirt for ease of movement at the organ. Surplice has semi-wing sleeves
Preaching bands	usually 14cm-20cm long
Preaching stoles	worn over the surplice and secured by a small chain in front, stoles are usually 127cm long. Until recently, stoles when worn over an alb were crossed at the front by priests and uncrossed by bishops. They are usually worn uncrossed today
Preaching scarves or Tippets	usually gathered at the neck with pinked ends, can be made ungathered and/or with plain ends. Length according to height of wearer. Black for priests, blue for readers
Vergers' gowns	can have divided sleeves and open front for maximum movement and comfort or can have a close front with velveteen trimmings, collar and epaulettes

Latin   Glory   Sovereignty   Calvary

Passion   Celtic   Iona   Cross & Thorny Crown

Saltire   Fimbriated   Adorned   Easter

Russian Orthodox   Lorraine   Patriarchal   Papal

St Peter's   St James's   Christus Rex   Crucifix

CROSSES

49

CROSSES
Terms

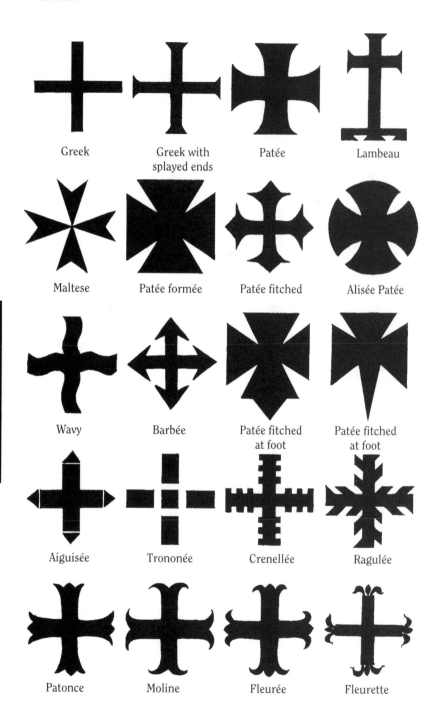

Greek

Greek with
splayed ends

Patée

Lambeau

Maltese

Patée formée

Patée fitched

Alisée Patée

Wavy

Barbée

Patée fitched
at foot

Patée fitched
at foot

Aiguisée

Trononée

Crenellée

Ragulée

Patonce

Moline

Fleurée

Fleurette

CROSSES

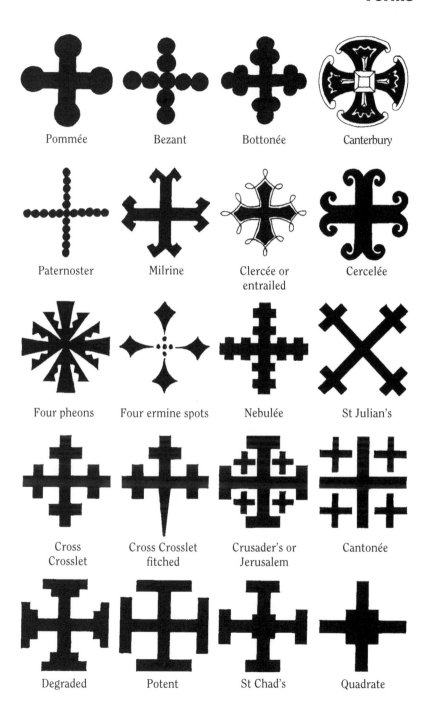

Pommée

Bezant

Bottonée

Canterbury

Paternoster

Milrine

Clercée or entrailed

Cercelée

Four pheons

Four ermine spots

Nebulée

St Julian's

Cross Crosslet

Cross Crosslet fitched

Crusader's or Jerusalem

Cantonée

Degraded

Potent

St Chad's

Quadrate

CROSSES

51

CROSSES
Terms

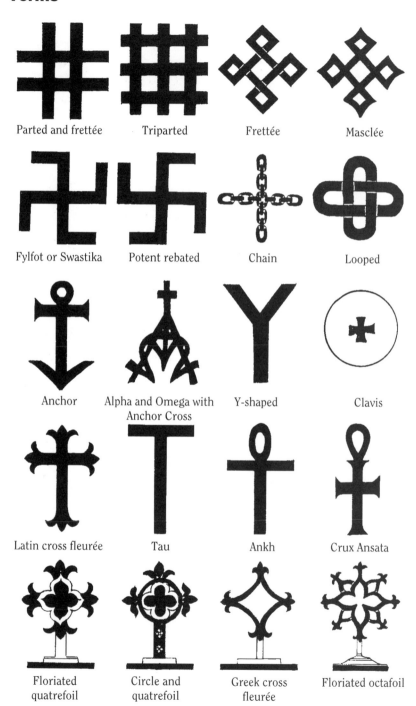

Parted and frettée

Triparted

Frettée

Masclée

Fylfot or Swastika

Potent rebated

Chain

Looped

Anchor

Alpha and Omega with
Anchor Cross

Y-shaped

Clavis

Latin cross fleurée

Tau

Ankh

Crux Ansata

Floriated
quatrefoil

Circle and
quatrefoil

Greek cross
fleurée

Floriated octafoil

TERMS

Crucifix	cross with the image of Christ affixed
Crucifix of Christus Rex	crucifix with Christ figure in eucharistic vestments and crown
Christ in Agony	crucifix figure with open eyes
Corpus Christi or The Dead Christ	crucifix figure with closed eyes

Ivory corpus Christi screwed onto oak Latin cross with bevelled edges. Bearded head, with closed eyes, crowned with thorns and bowed to the right arms upstretched and fingers clasped; slightly curved torso with loose **perizonium** *(loin cloth)* knotted over right hip; right knee bent; feet superimposed but nailed separately. Ivory scroll super-inscription or **titulus** attached with brass nail

DECORATION
Friezes

Decorative friezes and motifs may appear on a variety of objects in a variety of materials as architectural mouldings, embroidery, painted decoration or carving.

Acanthus

Anthemion

Ball flower

Ball flower and dogtooth

Bay Leaf

Bead

Bead and reel (Roman)

Bead and reel (Greek)

Beakhead

Bifurcated

Billet (round)

Billet (square)

Billet (alternate)

Brattishing

Cable

Chevron

Dentil (straight or diagonal)

Diaper

Dog tooth

Double cone

Egg and tongue

Egg and dart

Embattled

Enriched chevron

Festoon

Fleur-de-Lys

Four leaf flower

Fret or lattice or key or meander

Gadrooning, lobing or nulling

Goughing, chanelling or adzed (usually called scoop)

Guilloche

Husk

Imbricated interrupted by Tudor ornament

Interlacing *(resembling strapwork and moresque)*

Knotwork

Lotus alternating with palmette

Lozenge

Lunette

Meander

Moresque *(16th century term for interlacing)*

Nailhead

Ovolo *(convex moulding)*

DECORATION
Friezes

Patera (pl. patrae)

Peardrop

Pellet

Plait

Reeding and fluting

Ribbon or riband

Rosette *(rose patterned patera)*

Scalloped

Scratchwork and chipcarving

Scroll *(many variations)*

Shell

Star

Strapwork

Swag

Tracery (blind or applied)

Trellis or lattice

Trilobed foliage

Tudor ornament

Tudor rose

Vine

Vitruvian scroll or running dog

Waterleaf

(further examples on page 64)

Basketwork medallion

Grotesque

Bucranium

Mask

Chinoiserie medallion

Medallions

Cusp
(projecting point where foils meet)

Roundel

Foils: trefoil quatrefoil, cinque-, sex-, etc

Guttae
(truncated cones or triangles)

Foliation

Pendant

Floriation

Cherub, putto or amorino

Flory and counterflory

DECORATION
Flora and Fauna

Fruits, flowers, trees and figures may have symbolic meaning (see ATTRIBUTES & ALLEGORY) or may simply serve a decorative purpose.

Acacia   Acanthus   Almond   Anemone

Apple   Bay   Bramble   Bullrush

Carnation   Cherry   Christmas Rose   Clover

Columbine   Daisy   Dandelion   Glastonbury thorn

Grapes and vine   Holly   Iris   Ivy

Laurel

Lily

Lily of the valley

Love in the mist

Myrtle

Narcissus

Oak

Olive

Palm

Passion flower

Pear

Pomegranate

Poppy

Wild rose

Strawberry

Thistle

Tulip

Violet

Waterlily

Wheat or corn

DECORATION
Flora and Fauna

Antelope, hind,
hart, doe or stag

Basilisk or
cockatrice

Centaur

Dragon

Wyvern

Griffin

Dolphin

Phoenix

Salamander

Unicorn

Woodwose

Green man

Tree of Jesse

A branched tree with incorporated figures which combines the prophecy of Isaiah with the genealogical descent of Christ from Jesse (Matthew, ch 1). The figures on the branches represent the Prophets, often in contemporary dress, and the kings of Judah in the line of David. The Blessed Virgin Mary appears near the apex, holding the Child or with the figure of Christ above her and either the descending Dove of the Holy Spirit or doves representing the Gifts of the Holy Spirit.

Tree of Life

A naturalistic representation as a symbol of life, knowledge and salvation

Tree of life

Scroll frieze
14th century

DECORATION
Frames

Every edging, rim, border etc which encloses something is a frame. Frames are usually decorative and may be features in themselves. The same term is used for the skeleton of a piece of furniture.

Architectural frames   used for doors, windows, panels, tablets, medallions, niches, soffits, pictures, books etc

Cartouche   frame in the shape of a scroll of parchment with turned up ends

Frame   encloses a space with symmetrical decoration

Partial frame   external ornament top and bottom to emphasise the vertical, the lower ornament having the general shape of a bracket and the upper making a cresting feature

Strapwork frame   use of strapwork to surround or partially surround object; characteristic of Renaissance style, frequently with additional foliage and festoons. In books, and on monuments, strapwork often includes architectural forms

Partial frame

Frame

Cartouche

Ribbon scrolls

Strapwork bookplate

Diptych

wing   centre panel   wing

Triptych

Wall paintings

Painted mural decoration was common in pre-Reformation churches in Britain and constantly replaced and renewed. In the mid 16th century, many wall paintings were obliterated and some were overpainted with texts (**The Sentences**). In the 20th century some medieval paintings have been restored from beneath limewashing and overpainting. Subject matter was more important than artistic merit and few painters, except those working for royalty, are known.

Fresco painting onto damp plaster, usually employed in Italy but rarely in Britain.

Secco painting onto dry plaster, usually in red, yellow, white and black, commonly employed in Britain. Paintings applied by this method have a tendency to flake off the wall.

Wall paintings should be read as a strip cartoon; they are sometimes in two or more tiers, the individual scenes being divided by architectural motifs or bordered top and bottom. Incidents are often telescoped so that figures at the end of one scene may be back to back with the figures in the next. Scenes are stylised. Good people have haloes; bad people are caricatured; accessories are enlarged out of proportion to emphasise rank, authority or cruelty. Costume is usually contemporary and will give a clue to the date of the work. Souls are usually naked figures but carry rank identifications *(see ATTRIBUTES & ALLEGORY)*. Subjects group into four types:

Decorative masonry patterns

12th/14th centuries: scroll, chevron, heraldry, vine, diapering

14th/15th centuries: decoration characterised by clear stencilling

Bible stories including the Tree of Life and Tree of Jesse

Saints, apostles, martyrs and scenes from their lives

Moralities or allegorical themes containing warnings against particular sins or modes of life including the Seven Deadly Sins, the Seven Works of Mercy, the Weighing of Souls and the Doom or Last Judgement.

The Doom

Christ, robed to display the Five Wounds, seated on a rainbow, judging the living and dead. He blesses with one hand and holds up an open palm of judgement with the other. His feet rest on a sphere. He is flanked by groups of the Heavenly Host, Apostles, Evangelists, the Virgin Mary and St John the Baptist. Angels bear the Symbols of the Passion or blow trumpets. **Scrolls** often bear *Come ye blessed of my Father and inherit your Kingdom* on His right and *Go ye evil doers into eternal fire* on His left. Lower down, in the general resurrection St Peter receives the Blessed at the gate of Heaven and the sinners are damned in Hell.

Owl and Magpie copied from a Bestiary illustrating *idle chatterers mocking wisdom* c1330

Trophy *(decorative group of weapons, musical instruments or armour usually displayed with foliations, ribbons and flowers)*

DECORATION
Walls

Masons' marks
Distinguishing marks incised in stonework to identify the craftsman who worked it. Complex marks may have illustrated the pedigree of the mason, others were simple identifications for payment. Position marks indicated the order in which the stones were to be set

Vertebrate band (*continuous design, usually of flowers, fruit or foilage with the main stem running through the centre*)

Rinceau band (*similar to vertebrate, but with a wavy central stem*)

Allegorical vine border
13th century

Pelta or double axe pattern, c1100

Graffiti can be inscriptions, shapes, figures, or even music, scratched or cut in the fabric or furnishings of a building. In a church they occur chiefly in stone or plaster surfaces

Consecration crosses
usually twelve within church (painted) and twelve without (carved)

Medieval graffiti may be of considerable interest and should be recorded carefully with the help of torch and magnifying glass. Take measurements, including height from the floor, and give the location and any historical information (as distinct from imaginative interpretation). Each graffito can be illustrated by a sketch, a photograph (side-lit), or a rubbing made with soft pencil. Categories often include: objects drawn for votive purposes; crosses made by pilgrims and others; a priest's name and his induction date on chancel doorways; circles and compass-drawn motifs marking sites of consecration crosses; outline drawings on which mural paintings were based; portraits and caricatures; sketches for a craftsman's work, eg window tracery; staves of music (at points where processional singing took place)

A knowledge of the basic principles of heraldry will help in understanding monuments, stained glass windows, kneelers and embroidered banners.

Heraldic decoration can be described either by **blazoning** *(using correct heraldic terminology)* or **tricking** *(making a rough sketch with a detailed description of colours and motifs)* (see page 76). To identify a particular coat of arms it may help to look for another elsewhere in the church or graveyard under which there might be a helpful inscription. Church leaflets, the incumbent, local antiquarian societies and the local reference library will be helpful. It is impossible to trace every coat of arms, particularly those assumed improperly in Victorian times.

Women may display badges but are not entitled to display their arms on a shield nor are they permitted a helm or crest. They may display their arms on a lozenge or cartouche. The personal arms of a bishop are impaled with the arms of his See; a rule which also applies to certain office holders.

Achievement	the complete armorial device, including shield, helm, crest, mantling, wreath, supporters, motto, etc. Usually referred to as **armorials** on plate (see page 119)
Badge	device denoting membership of a community, or strictly personal addition to coat of arms; borne by soldiers and servants of the medieval household
Base	bottom of shield
Chief	top of shield
Coat of Arms	displayed on the shield, lozenge or banner
Crest	device borne on the top of the helm
Crest coronet	may replace crest wreath
Crest wreath or torse	wreath hiding joint between crest and helm
Dexter	left side as viewed from the front
Field	ground of shield
Hatchment	the armorial bearings of a deceased person, usually painted on canvas stretched across a lozenge-shaped frame, heavily painted to withstand the weather
Helm	helmet above shield, different according to rank
Impaled	arrangement of two coats of arms side by side on one shield
Insignia	distinguishing mark of an office or honour
Mantling or lambrequin	a short mantle fixed to and flowing from the top of the helm
Shield	central heraldic device bearing arms; varied in shape but variance of no significance
Sinister	right side as viewed from the front

HERALDRY
Terms

Crest

Mural Crown (alternative to wreath, torse or crest coronet)

Mantling

Helm

Supporters

Shield

Compartment

Motto on scroll

SEMPER·COMMUNITAS

Crest

Crest wreath or torse

Helm

Mantling

Shield

Gauntlets

Spurs

Sword

Badge

Chapeau

Armorial accessories
as displayed in churches

SHIELD SHAPES

Kite Triangular À Spade
or heater bouche

POINTS OF THE SHIELD

QUARTERINGS

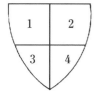

The numbering and
precedence of a simple
quartered shield

*Record the total number of
quarterings together with
the blazon or tricking
of each quarter*

Per pale Or and
Gu. three roundels
counterchanged

DIVISIONS OF THE FIELD

Per fess

Per pale

Per bend

Per bend
sinister

Per chevron

Per pall

Per saltire

Quarterly

VARIED FIELDS

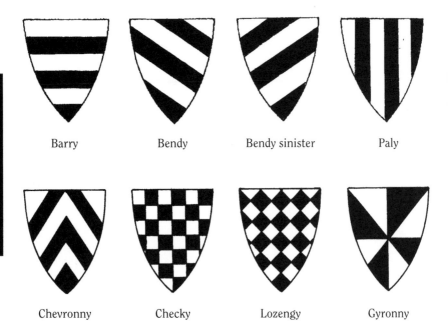

Barry	Bendy	Bendy sinister	Paly
Chevronny	Checky	Lozengy	Gyronny

The field may be varied by division with geometric lines eg paly of six Argent and Azure, describes six vertical stripes alternately silver and blue. The lines may be plain or decorated

If tinctures of the field or charges are reversed on either side of a line of partition, they are said to be counterchanged (see page 67)

Escutcheon of pretence

indicates marriage to an heraldic heiress

The distinguishing mark for baronets (except of Nova Scotia). A white shield charged with a sinister open hand couped at the wrist, Gules

VARIED LINES

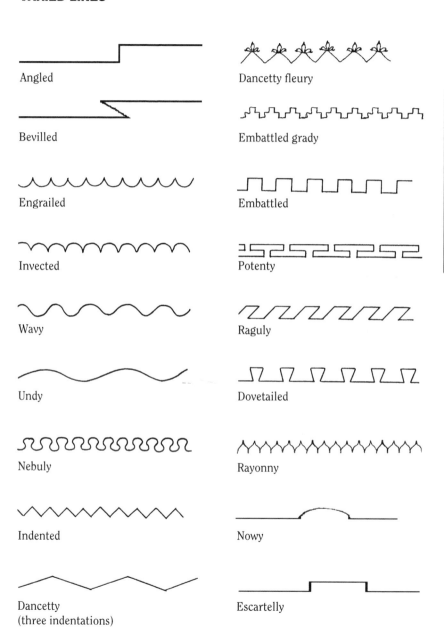

Angled

Bevilled

Engrailed

Invected

Wavy

Undy

Nebuly

Indented

Dancetty
(three indentations)

Dancetty fleury

Embattled grady

Embattled

Potenty

Raguly

Dovetailed

Rayonny

Nowy

Escartelly

HERALDRY
The Shield

TINCTURES & HATCHINGS

There is an exact terminology for armorial tinctures which will be indicated in records by the following hatchings. As a general rule a device of a colour should not be placed on a field of a colour, nor a metal on metal, nor fur on fur. However there are exceptions to this rule.

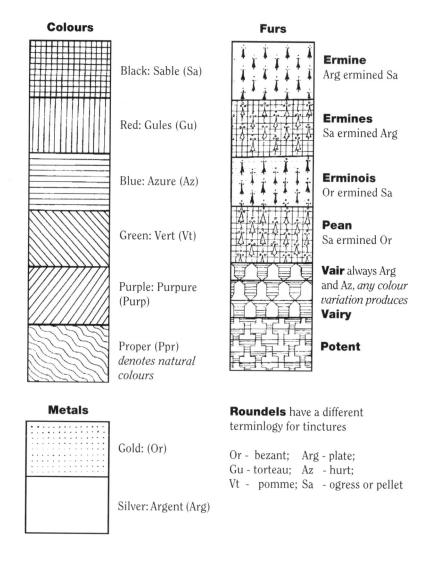

Colours

Black: Sable (Sa)

Red: Gules (Gu)

Blue: Azure (Az)

Green: Vert (Vt)

Purple: Purpure (Purp)

Proper (Ppr) *denotes natural colours*

Metals

Gold: (Or)

Silver: Argent (Arg)

Furs

Ermine
Arg ermined Sa

Ermines
Sa ermined Arg

Erminois
Or ermined Sa

Pean
Sa ermined Or

Vair always Arg and Az, *any colour variation produces*
Vairy

Potent

Roundels have a different terminlogy for tinctures

Or - bezant;   Arg - plate;
Gu - torteau;   Az - hurt;
Vt - pomme;   Sa - ogress or pellet

CHARGES AND ORDINARIES

Charges are any objects or figures placed on a shield. Charges may be geometrical (the **ordinaries** and **sub-ordinaries**) or any other device, animate or inanimate.

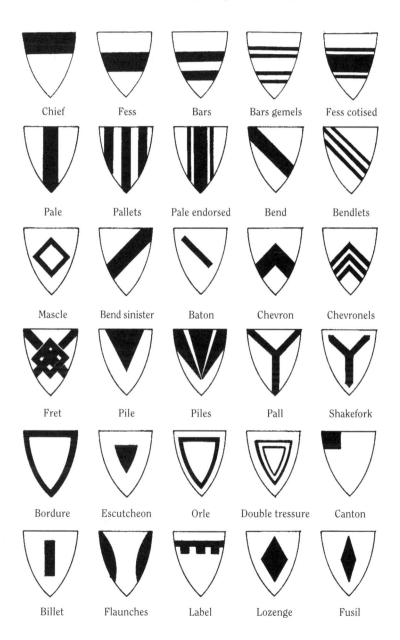

Chief	Fess	Bars	Bars gemels	Fess cotised
Pale	Pallets	Pale endorsed	Bend	Bendlets
Mascle	Bend sinister	Baton	Chevron	Chevronels
Fret	Pile	Piles	Pall	Shakefork
Bordure	Escutcheon	Orle	Double tressure	Canton
Billet	Flaunches	Label	Lozenge	Fusil

HERALDRY

HERALDRY
The Shield

ATTITUDES

The attitudes of living creatures should be described. The terminology of attitudes for lions is shown below. Terminology varies for other animals.

Rampant	Rampant guardant	Rampant reguardant	Salient
Statant guardant	Passant	Sejant	Couchant
Dormant	Lions addorsed	Lions combatant	Lion rampant double-headed

CADENCY MARKS

Denote seniority in a family and sometimes distinguish one branch from another.

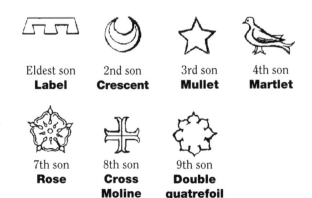

Eldest son	2nd son	3rd son	4th son	5th son	6th son
Label	**Crescent**	**Mullet**	**Martlet**	**Annulet**	**Fleur-de-Lys**

7th son	8th son	9th son
Rose	**Cross Moline**	**Double quatrefoil**

HELMS

King and royal family
gold, six bars affrontée

Baronet or knight
steel, vizor raised, affrontée

Earl, peer or baron
silver, garnished with gold four or five bars, (shown facing the dexter)

Gentleman or esquire
steel, vizor closed, (shown facing the dexter)

CROWNS & CORONETS

Between the helm and the crest is either a **wreath** or a **cap of maintenance** (or **chapeau**) or a **crest coronet** (see page 66). This may be a **ducal coronet** of fleurs-de-lys (nothing to do with dukes), a **naval** or a **mural crown**.

Crowns which appear elsewhere, apart from Crowns of Rank, include the **Eastern** and the **Celestial crown**.

Naval crown

Eastern crown

Ducal crown

Celestial crown

HERALDRY
Crowns and Coronets of Rank

Duke's coronet
Eight strawberry leaves of equal height, five visible

Royal crown
(worn by King and King's heir). Four crosses patée alternating with fleurs-de-lys

King's crown has diadems springing from the crosses and the junction is surmounted by a mount bearing another cross patée

Heir's crown is similar but with only two diadems

Marquess's coronet
Four strawberry leaves alternating with four pearls of equal height, three leaves and two pearls visible

Earl's coronet
Eight pearls on long points alternating with eight short strawberry leaves, five pearls and four leaves visible

Viscount's coronet
Sixteen pearls on rim, eight or nine pearls visible

Royal coronet worn by younger sons and brothers of kings similar to royal crown but without diadems and cross, surmounted by golden tassel

Baron's coronet
Six pearls on rim, four visible

The heraldry of hatchments is not always accurate and the motto not always that of the family; silver and gold are indicated by white and yellow. The dexter side is the male side, except for bishops and others holding certain public office. The background is always black behind the arms of the deceased. Variations occur when the arms of more than one wife are depicted.

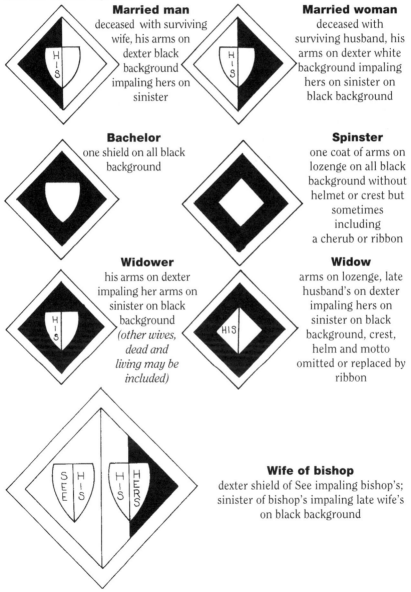

Married man
deceased with surviving wife, his arms on dexter black background impaling hers on sinister

Married woman
deceased with surviving husband, his arms on dexter white background impaling hers on sinister on black background

Bachelor
one shield on all black background

Spinster
one coat of arms on lozenge on all black background without helmet or crest but sometimes including a cherub or ribbon

Widower
his arms on dexter impaling her arms on sinister on black background *(other wives, dead and living may be included)*

Widow
arms on lozenge, late husband's on dexter impaling hers on sinister on black background, crest, helm and motto omitted or replaced by ribbon

Wife of bishop
dexter shield of See impaling bishop's; sinister of bishop's impaling late wife's on black background

Skull in place of crest is said to indicate the extinction of a family

HERALDRY
Hatchments

BLAZONING
Hatchment of Donald Cameron of Lochiel d1858

Hatchment: dexter black
Gu three bars Or impaling Sa an estoile of eight rays Or between two flaunches Erm (Hobart)

Crest: a dexter arm embowed in armour, the hand grasping a sword, all Ppr

Supporters: two savages, wreathed head and middle with oak, each holding in his exterior hand a Lochabar axe, all Ppr

Mantling: Or and Gu
Motto under: PRO REGE ET PATRIA

TRICKING
Hatchment of Donald Cameron of Lochiel d1858

Hatchment

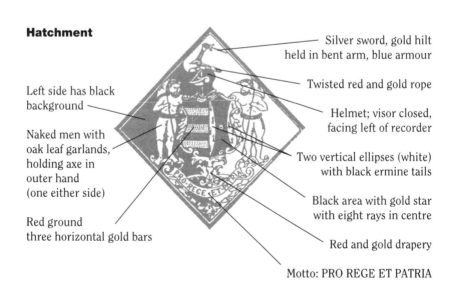

Silver sword, gold hilt held in bent arm, blue armour

Twisted red and gold rope

Left side has black background

Helmet; visor closed, facing left of recorder

Naked men with oak leaf garlands, holding axe in outer hand (one either side)

Two vertical ellipses (white) with black ermine tails

Black area with gold star with eight rays in centre

Red ground three horizontal gold bars

Red and gold drapery

Motto: PRO REGE ET PATRIA

pre 1340
Gules, three lions passant guardant in pale Or

1340-1405
1 & 4 France
2 & 3 England

1405-1603
1 & 4 France modern
2 & 3 England

1603-1707
1 & 4 quarterly France and England
2 Scotland
(Or, a lion rampant within a double tressure flory counterflory Gu)
3 Ireland
(Az a harp Or, stringed Arg)

1689-1702
1 & 4 quarterly France and England
2 Scotland
3 Ireland
Escutcheon: arms of Nassau (Az billety charged with a lion rampant Or)

1707-1714
1 & 4 England impaling Scotland
2 France modern
3 Ireland

1714-1801
1 England impaling Scotland
2 France modern
3 Ireland
4 Hanover

1801-1816
1 & 4 England
2 Scotland
3 Ireland
Escutcheon: arms of Hanover ensigned with electoral cap

1816-37
1 & 4 England
2 Scotland
3 Ireland
Escutcheon: arms of Hanover ensigned with crown

HERALDRY
Royal Arms

1837 onwards
Arms

quarterly, 1st and 4th (England), Gu three lions pass. guard. in pale Or 2nd (Scotland) Or a lion rampant within a double tressure flory counterflory Gu 3rd (Ireland) Az a harp Or stringed Arg the whole encircled with the Garter

Crest	Upon the royal helmet, the imperial crown Ppr, thereon a lion statant guardant Or, imperially crowned Ppr
Supporters	Dexter, a lion ramp. guard., Or, crowned as the crest; sinister, an unicorn Arg armed, crined and unguled Or, gorged with a coronet composed of crosses patée and fleurs-de-lys, a chain affixed thereto, passing between the fore-legs and reflexed over the back Or
Motto	*DIEU ET MON DROIT* in the compartment below the shield; with the Union rose, shamrock and thistle engrafted on the same stem
Crown of England	a circle Or, issuing therefrom four crosses patée and four fleurs-de-lys, arranged alternately; from the crosses patée arise two arched diadems Or ornamented with pearls, closing at the top under a mound, surmounted by a cross patée also Or, the whole enriched with precious stones; cap of crimson velvet turned up Erm

Badges

England	red and white rose united
Scotland	thistle
Ireland	a harp Or, stringed Arg shamrock leaf Vert
Wales	dragon pass wings elevated Gu upon a mound Vert

All ensigned with the royal crown

A standard description 'Royal Arms as used from 1837' can be used to replace full blazoning

ORDERS OF KNIGHTHOOD

The symbols of orders will appear on the insignia and the arms will include the motto.

The Order of the Garter — with buckle
'Honi soit qui mal y pense'

The Order of the Thistle — saltire cross and thistle
'Nemo me impune lacessit'

The Order of St Patrick — shamrock
'Quis separabit'

The Order of the Bath — Maltese cross with rose, thistle and shamrock in centre
'Tria juncta in uno'

The Star of India — *'Heaven's light our guide'*

The Order of St Michael and St George — *'Auspicium Melioris Aevi'*

The Order of Victoria and Albert — Queen Victoria and Prince Albert in profile

ECCLESIASTICAL ARMS

Each See has its own arms. The chief provinces of the Church of England are the Archiepiscopal Sees of Canterbury and York. There is no helm or crest with personal arms of the clergy.

Canterbury
Az an archiepiscopal cross in pale Or surmounted by a pall Ppr charged with four crosses patée fitchée Sa

York
Gu two keys in saltire Arg in chief a regal crown

LETTERING
Terms

Lettering appears on memorials, in books and manuscripts, on stained and engraved glass and textiles. It is possible to consider a general approach to the classification of lettering but in addition, specific systems exist for the identification of silver, pewter and ceramics.

Applied individual letters cast or carved and pinned to the surface of buildings and memorials; commonly of gilded wood, brass, bronze and lead

Flat painted or gilded directly onto the surface; a fine outline may show around letters painted on stone

Incised cut into the surface. Letters may be painted in a colour or filled with lead or mastic

V-Cut Gouged Lowered Cushioned

Raised background cut away leaving letters in relief; may be raised, domed or raised with inline

Raised Domed Raised with inline

On manuscripts and in calligraphy, the capital and small letters are described as **majuscules** and **minuscules** respectively. However, printing has provided the widest terminology for describing letterforms. The terms **upper case** and **lower case** derive from the type cases of printers where the case of capital letters lies above that of small letters. Today, **capital letters** and **lower case** letters are the terms most generally understood WHEN DESCRIBING ALL LETTERING OTHER THAN MANUSCRIPTS.

Cap line
x height — NKG nkg — Ascender
Base line
Drop line — Descender
Serifs

Light Medium Bold Extra Bold

Weight described as **light; medium; bold** or **extra bold**

DISPLAYWORK STAR
Condensed Expanded

Width described as **condensed** or **expanded**
Latin Condensed type or Latin Expanded type

80

REPRO ADM
Decorated   Flourished

Decorated letters   elaborations of a **basic** form
Fry's Ornamented type

Flourished   part of the basic letter, either roman or italic
extended into a flourished shape
Perpetua type, italic capitals

ABCD   ABCab
Outlined   Shaded

Outlined/shaded   outlined or shaded to give the impression of a third
dimension
Grotesque Outline type or Chisel Shaded type

MP·CAES

Classical roman   the word **roman** has several meanings and it is
important to distinguish between them. During the 1st
century AD inscriptional lettering in Rome had its
greatest flowering. The Trajan inscription is one fine
example. The style of lettering which it portrays is
referred to as Classical roman

ABCEMORS
abcdefghimop

Roman   printing term denoting both capital and lower case
letters which are upright as opposed to sloped or italic
and which have their roots in the Classical roman
letters
Perpetua type, designed by Eric Gill

ABCEMORST
abcdefghimnop

Italic flourished version of sloped roman. The name stems from the letterforms of Italian writing masters of the 16th century

Sloped roman term used by letter designers for a plainer version of italic
Perpetua italic type

A B C a b c d ⌐

Sans serif letterforms characterised by a lack of serifs and a more even width of stroke throughout each letter. Within this group are types variously described as **Grotesque, Glyptic** and, confusingly, **Gothic** but sans serif is the simplest and most commonly used description

ABCabcd

Clarendon letters with bracketed serifs, derived from the typeface of that name. It is found incised on many 18th and 19th century gravestones

ABC abcd

Egyptian letters with square serifs, used extensively on memorials in various weights and sets
Rockwell type

ABCDEF
abcdefgh

Latin letters with triangular serifs
Latin Expanded type

𝔄 𝔅 ℭ 𝔞𝔟𝔠

Gothic
letters with strong vertical pen stress, evenly spaced elements and angular terminals with wide variations showing condensation, expansion, decoration and flourishing. Also known as **Black Letter** in medieval manuscripts
Old English type

Effect may be copied

Copper plate well known 18th century pen style
Marina Script type

MANUSCRIPT LETTERFORMS
Of the great variety of manuscript styles developed in Europe from the 1st century AD, these examples represent clear stages in the development of writing

RATESETMYSTICAVANN
AFAIVLIOANIEMEMORI

Majuscules or *Square capitals* from a 3rd century Virgil in the Vatican
Quadrata   Library, Cod Vat 3256

TESTATVAMORITVRADEOS
SIDERATVMSIQVODNONA

Rustica   or *Rustic capitals* from a 4th century Virgil in the Vatican Library, Cod Palat Lat 1631

fecerunt ocili,

Uncials   from 5th century manuscript in the British Library, Cotton MS Vespasian A i

abate bibere

Half uncials   from 7th century Lindisfarne Gospels, British Library, Cotton MS Nero D iv

LETTERING
Styles

R A L O M

Versals   based on a 7th century manuscript

hunc ab ordo mo

Roman Script script based on 9th century Carolingian pen writing,
Bodelian MS, ED Clarke 28

aboram damant

Gothic   Gothic book hand from 13th century York Psalter,
British Library 54179

delectatio afferretur

Italic   Early 16th century italic script Arrighi *(attributed)*,
British Library, Royal MS 12C VIII

TWO-DIMENSIONAL SHAPES

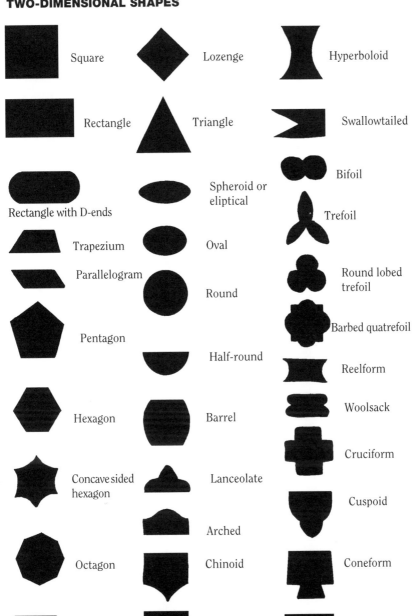

Square

Lozenge

Hyperboloid

Rectangle

Triangle

Swallowtailed

Rectangle with D-ends

Spheroid or eliptical

Bifoil

Trapezium

Oval

Trefoil

Parallelogram

Round

Round lobed trefoil

Pentagon

Half-round

Barbed quatrefoil

Hexagon

Barrel

Reelform

Concave sided hexagon

Lanceolate

Woolsack

Octagon

Arched

Cruciform

Plinthform

Chinoid

Cuspoid

Lobus

Coneform

Globoid

SHAPES AND MOULDINGS
Universal Shapes

THREE-DIMENSIONAL SHAPES

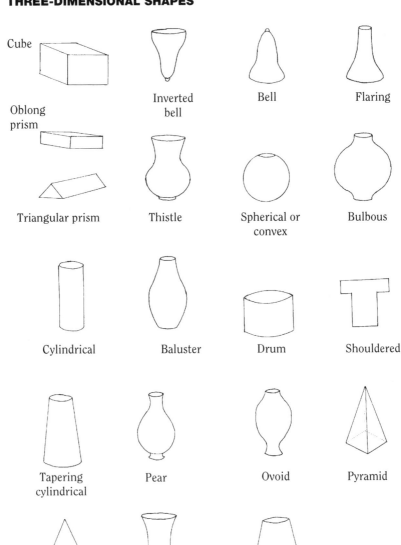

Cube

Oblong prism

Triangular prism

Inverted bell

Thistle

Bell

Spherical or convex

Flaring

Bulbous

Cylindrical

Baluster

Drum

Shouldered

Tapering cylindrical

Pear

Ovoid

Pyramid

Conical

Concave sided

Truncated cone

COMPLEX SHAPES

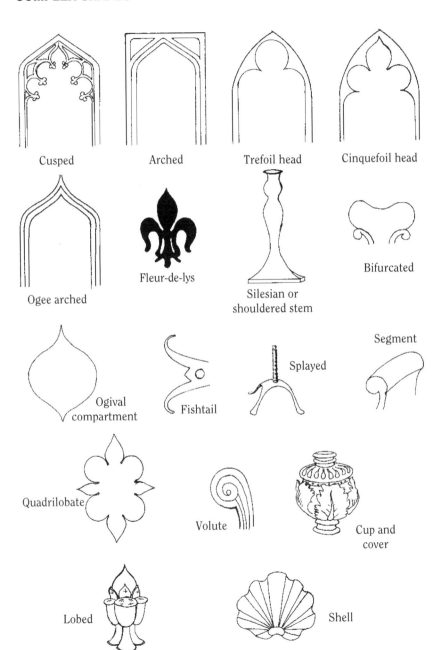

Cusped

Arched

Trefoil head

Cinquefoil head

Ogee arched

Fleur-de-lys

Silesian or
shouldered stem

Bifurcated

Ogival
compartment

Fishtail

Splayed

Segment

Quadrilobate

Volute

Cup and
cover

Lobed

Shell

SHAPES & MOULDINGS

87

SHAPES AND MOULDINGS
Cups, Plates and Jugs

Baluster
(or pear or
tulip)

Baluster

Squat baluster

(Pewter vessels: bulbous or bellied)

Bombe

Cylindrical

Tapering
cylindrical

(Pewter vessels: truncated cone)

Lip

Tall
cylindrical

Skirt

Tall tapering
cylindrical with
skirt

Barrel

Barrel

Boat

Drum

Helmet

Urn
(or vase or
ovoid)

Hexagonal
stepped stand or
socle

Plate-shaped

Dish-shaped or
basin-shaped

Bowl-shaped or
saucer-shaped

Cup-shaped

Flat

Pomegranate

Ball

Ring

Raised
flat-
topped

Bud

Crossed Patée
formée cross

Flame

Bun

Lobed

Crown

Bell

Cap

Dove

Banded
Knop

Urn

Beefeater

Lobed and
foliated

Acorn

Baluster

High
domed

Orb

Cone

Ball and
Steeple

Domed

Stepped
domed

Double
domed

Waisted

SHAPES AND MOULDINGS
Feet and Handles

Arcaded

High
circular

Tuck-in base
on spreading
rim

Stud

Incurving

Trumpet

Bun

Standard
or loop

Lobed
quatrefoil

Circular moulded
spreading

Ball

Angular

Shaped lobed
or wavy

Domed on
narrow
flange

Reeded base

Baluster

Paw

Spreading
skirt

Hexagonal
spreading moulded

Capped scroll

Cusped tripod

Shallow dome or
spreading conical

Shell and
scroll

Scroll

Stepped circular

High conical

Flying scroll

Broken or double
scroll

Baluster

Inverted Baluster

Reeded

Hexagonal Bud

Spherical

Compressed
or proper

Lobed

Wrythen or
spiralling

Hexagonal

Compressed
and annulated

Bladed
(or flange)

Wrythen
Gothic

Lobed Gothic

Lobed
flange

Compressed knot
above a flange

Swelling

Cup and cover
or melon

Shouldered

Mushroom

Dumb-bell

Cushioned

Cone

Acorn

Multi-knotted

SHAPES AND MOULDINGS
Mouldings

Mouldings are plain or enriched projecting or recessed bands of decoration either worked directly (**struck**) or **applied**

Bead and butt	moulding worked on two sides of panel
Bead and flush	moulding worked on all four sides of panel
Pulvinated	with cushion-like swelling
Quirk	groove running parallel to bead

The names of mouldings follow classical rules for all styles except gothic mouldings which have their own terminology, here represented in brackets where the moulding style exist

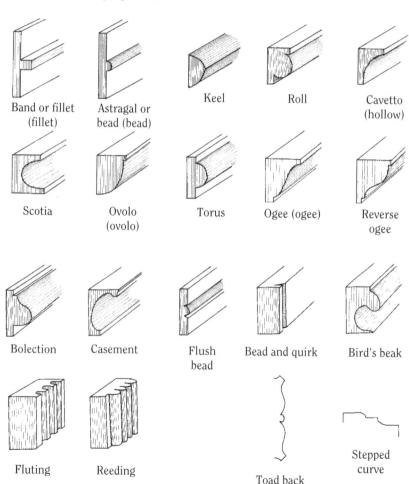

Band or fillet (fillet)

Astragal or bead (bead)

Keel

Roll

Cavetto (hollow)

Scotia

Ovolo (ovolo)

Torus

Ogee (ogee)

Reverse ogee

Bolection

Casement

Flush bead

Bead and quirk

Bird's beak

Fluting

Reeding

Toad back

Stepped curve

MATERIALS

CERAMICS
Marks

Ceramics include objects made of porcelain and pottery. Ceramics other than tiles are not common in churches but are occasionally encountered, possibly an early pottery jug or a china vase. Even a cracked 18th century piece may be of value. If you do find a ceramic piece you will probably need a detailed reference book. *See FURTHER READING.*

PORCELAIN   is *translucent* unless the body is very thick. The body is white and almost invariably has a transparent glaze, which may be slightly blued. Vases etc. are glazed inside and out

POTTERY   is *opaque,* the clay body varying from brown, grey, red, orange to white. When the body is not white, a white opaque glaze may be used to imitate porcelain. The clay body is porous so has to be glazed, at least on the inside, if it is to hold liquid

MARKS

Many ceramic pieces are marked, usually on the base, with the factory mark and/ or the decorator's or potter's marks. These marks are found both under the glaze and over the glaze and may be painted, printed, incised or impressed. Since in the 18th and 19th centuries many factories copied the marks of other factories, marks alone are unreliable for attribution purposes.

Make a note of the mark, if there is one, and consult your local museum or someone knowledgeable on ceramics if you think the piece is of interest.

Between 1842 and 1883 a registration mark was used by many manufacturers in the UK which gave copyright protection.

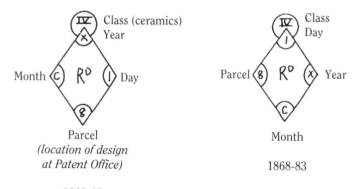

1842-67

1868-83

A simple registration number only was used from 1884-1901

An item marked *'England'* dates from 1891 or later, an item marked *'Made in England'* dates from the 20th century

Here are a few marks commonly found on ceramics in English houses which may have found their way into churches.

Meissen but copied and adapted by numerous factories

Bow, Chelsea, Derby, Venice, or 19th century copies all used an anchor mark but the shape may vary

Derby c1785-1830 similar marks in red, blue or purple, or incised

18th century English soft paste typical fancy outline used by Victorian factories, usually incorporating the pattern name and number

Wedgwood
note the full mark, lettering and spelling, as other firms using the name, often spelt Wedgewood, would not be genuine

18th century **Sparrow Beak** jug, small with ribbed, smooth or patterned surfaces

Mid 19th century **Dragon Vase** with six-character mark of *K'ang Hsi* dynasty. Globular body and cylindrical neck, decorated with nine scaly five-clawed dragons, all of different colour and with ferocious expressions, on a ground of white crested waves painted in underglaze blue

Record the mark accurately and in detail with a photograph or drawing and a note of the shape, glaze, colour and design. Recognise the difference between underglaze and decoration over the glaze. Record even unmarked underglaze items. Anything handpainted, unless obviously of amateur workmanship, is of interest

CERAMICS
Floor Tiles

MEDIEVAL FLOOR TILES

Plain tiles
Plain lead glazed earthenware tiles were probably introduced in the 12th century and were made in various sizes. Glazed with a lead glaze applied direct to the body or over white-slip or with added copper, the tiles were brown, yellow, or green to black. Yellow and green/black tiles were often laid chequerwise. Such hand-made plain glazed tiles are still in use

Mosaic tiles
Plain glazed mosaic may have been introduced as early as 1180 but most was made during the 13th century. Most arrangements were formed with rectilinear shapes but more intricate arrangements, including elaborate shapes, were used in important parts of the church. Yellow and green/black tiles were used alternately. Decoration was added to some elements of the mosaic arrangements from the 1230s, relief, linear or two-colour motifs being employed. All decorative designs were applied to the surface of the tile with a carved wooden stamp when the unfired tile was leather hard. The making of all mosaics was labour intensive and they were never mass-produced, few being made after the 1340s

Relief tiles
Relief decoration, either upstanding or depressed, was introduced in the late 12th century and continued in use until the 16th century and until the 18th century in Devon. Each tile was glazed a single colour, brown, yellow, green or black. Pavements were sometimes laid in alternating colours, sometimes in one colour only

Line-impressed tiles
During the early 14th century to the 16th century linear decoration was stamped on monochrome tiles. These also were laid either in alternating colours or in one colour only

Two-colour tiles
These tiles were introduced in the 1230s at first for special commissions but by the 1260s were also mass-produced. They became the most popular type and were made until the mid-16th century. As with the monochrome tiles the design was stamped on the surface of the leather hard tile with a wooden stamp on which the design was upstanding. The cavities so formed were filled with white firing clay introduced in various ways. On the earlier 'inlaid' tiles the white clay was pressed in a plastic state and in the later 15th and the 16th centuries it was often poured in as liquid slip. Other methods, less easily recognised, were also used. Both specially commissioned and mass-produced two-colour tiles were made throughout the period except for a few decades after the Black Death when few if any special tiles were commissioned

The best documented tilery was operating at Penn in Buckinghamshire from the 1330s to the 1380s. During this period its tiles were widely distributed in neighbouring counties and as far away as Kent and Surrey. There were certainly many more such tileries for which no records survive. The two-colour tiles were those most commonly reproduced during the Gothic revival

Fleur-de-lys between four quadrants, each enclosing an embattled quadrant and a quarter octofoil (Penn)

Design based on the Solomon's Seal with a quatrefoil at the centre within a star (Penn)

Part of a four-tile design of formal foliage in a quatrefoil, with foliage and fleurs-de-lys cut out by a quadrant in the outer angles. Surface damaged in two places (Wessex)

A repeating four-tile design of cinquefoils within circles powdered with lozenges, set in a square with foliated motifs in the spandrels and centre, alternating with squares enclosing conjoined fleurs-de-lys (Wessex)

CERAMICS
Floor Tiles

VICTORIAN FLOOR TILES

Quarry tiles Although this term is often applied to a wide range of plain floor tiles it is correctly used only for tiles which are moulded, cut or extruded from plastic (or wet) clay and unglazed. These tiles were much used in Victorian times for the aisles of churches and were usually laid in chequer patterns using red and black or red and buff tiles. The most common size is 15cm square but 10cm and 22.5cm were also used. Mainly produced in the Potteries and Wales, these tiles often have a coarse surface which contrasts with the smooth flat surface of dustpressed tiles

Dustpressed tiles In 1840, Richard Prosser of Birmingham patented a method of producing ceramic buttons by drying clay to a fine dust which was then put in a powerful press, thus forming the button rapidly and accurately. Herbert Minton bought a share in the patent and realised that the process could be applied to the manufacture of tiles and by 1842 was producing smooth flat floor tiles in several colours. Because they were easier to clean than quarry tiles they soon became very popular and were used in the same way as quarry tiles or to form surrounds for encaustic tiles *(see below)*. As well as squares, many other shapes were made which were usually based on geometric portions of a 15cm square and these were laid utilising the many colours in large mosaic designs known as **Geometric Pavements**

Encaustic tiles Herbert Minton produced reproductions of medieval encaustic tiles for use in Gothic Revival restorations from about 1835. Victorian encaustic tiles are easily recognized as they are usually far more precise and mechanical in design and manufacture than their predecessors. By 1860 many new colours had been introduced, often as many as eight on a single tile. Early tiles are normally unglazed or glazed over the inlay only, using a yellow majolica glaze. Later tiles, from about 1850 onwards, usually have a clear glaze or are fired to a higher (vitreous) temperature which makes them much less porous. Victorian encaustic tiles are quite often marked with the makers' name on the back and sometimes a **trade tile** was included which gives the makers' name and address. Common makers' names are Minton, Maw, Godwin, Craven Dunnill and Campbell

Opus Sectile Made from fragments of flint-glass contaminated with clay, ground to a fine powder and baked. It has an egg-shell finish and is suitable for wall tiles and mosaic, the range of colours is unlimited. Widely used in the 1880s for church memorials and decorative wall effects

Fourfold foliate design in quatrefoil. Block printed in black on white body under clear glaze. Manufactured by MINTON HOLLINS & CO (Minton & Co) c1845. Prossers Patent Dustpressed Method. (Marks moulded on reverse)

Sacred Monogram IHS interlaced in stylised barbed quatrefoil with quarter roses at corners. Red, white, yellow, orange, mauve and blue majolica glazes on dustpressed body. MINTON & CO c1855 (Marks moulded on reverse)

Encaustic tile with design of St George on horseback based on a medieval original from the Temple Church, London. Design adapted by A W N Pugin for Herbert Minton c1850 (MINTON & CO impressed on reverse) unglazed

Pseudo-medieval encaustic tile with cinquefoil in white and stylized foliate corners. Surface distressed to represent medieval tile. W GODWIN c1865 (Impressed marks on reverse) Worn glaze

METAL
Terms

There are metal objects all around churches, some are precious, some workaday; some are functional, some merely decorative; some have much in common with ceramics, some with wooden objects, some with stone.

Various aspects of metal objects are of interest, their use, the metal they are made of, the marks, armorials and inscriptions they bear, their size and date. Decoration, particularly in medieval work, often demonstrates the same features and style as contemporary architecture.

TYPES OF METAL

Bell metal   alloy of copper and tin

Brass   alloy of copper and zinc

Britannia metal hard form of pewter, appears similar to silver or polished pewter, it is produced in sheet form and thus permits cold processing of the metal such as spinning, die-stamping and hand-forming. In use from the 1780's until present day

Britannia silver 95.8 per cent pure silver

Bronze   alloy of copper, tin and other metal

Electroplate   method of laying fine particles of silver onto base metal, introduced in 1840's

EPBM   electroplated Britannia metal (after 1850). Makers' names and catalogue numbers may be found impressed into metal

EPGS   electroplated German silver (electroplated nickel silver)

EPNS   electroplated nickel silver, from c1840

Nickel silver alloy of copper, zinc and nickel, often passed off as silver by mis-describing nickel eg German silver

Ormolu   gilded bronze or copper alloy, mostly used for mounts

Parcel gilt   silver with part coating of gold

Pewter   greyish alloy of tin with small amounts of lead and/or copper and/or antimony. Bright like silver when new but oxidises with time to grey appearance. Makers' marks often found (see page 103)

Sheffield plate copper sandwiched and fused between layers of sterling silver and rolled into sheets for use, made from 1760-1840. Seams are dovetailed and edges often rolled to disguise the sandwich. Marks, when found, are similar to hallmarks on early pieces, later a manufacturer's name or symbol may be indented

Silver gilt   silver with coating of gold

Silver plate   utensils of silver

Silver plated articles of metal with thin coating of silver

Sterling standard 92.5 per cent silver

DECORATIVE TECHNIQUES

Annulated   decorated with rings

Applied   ornament or part overlaid onto a surface

Cast   pattern made by running molten metal into a mould

Chasing   metal decorated by means of hammer-blows pushing along a punch to indent a pattern

Embossing or repoussé   metal hammered from the back to form bosses or raised patterns. Often used in conjunction with chasing

Enamelling   enamel is finely ground glass, coloured by metallic oxides, fused by heat to a metal surface. It may be matte or gloss, opaque, translucent or opalescent

The various kinds of enamelling include:

Basse-taille   level-topped layer of transparent enamel laid over sculptured and chased metal in low relief, with consequent variation in the depth of colour

Champlevé   recesses in the metal ground are filled with enamel

Cloisonné   cells of wire or narrow strips of metal, on a metal ground enclose areas of colour

Dipped   enamelling in the round, found on sculpture and jewellery

Painted   a metal foundation, usually slightly domed, enamelled overall on both sides, then brush-decorated, often over a transfer print

Plique-à-jour   *(light of day)*: pierced metal or cloissons hold transparent enamels so that light passes through like stained-glass

Printed   transfer or bat-printed, usually monochrome on a plain enamelled ground

Engraving   removal of metal by sharp tools, used particularly for lettering and armorials (early 18th century armorials **cast, chased or applied**)

Finial   decorative knob on top of lid, cover or upright etc or terminal at base of handle

Hatched/matted   engraved lines, small circles or dots produced by a hollow punch

Knot/Knop   protrusion on stem

Niello   engraved lines or depressions filled with black composition

Swan-necked handle   double curving feature similar to scrolling

Thumbpiece   finial rising from top of handle to be held by the thumb

Reed   ring cast on or near the outside edge of a pewter plate

Wriggle-work   method of decorating or drawing on pewter by rocking the end of a chisel or other tool backwards and forwards to produce zig-zag lines

METAL
Marks

Metal marks generally consist of a **maker's mark**; a **metal mark**; for precious metals, an **Assay Office Mark**; and a **date letter**. A detailed pocket guide to marks is an essential tool. The first mark is the Sponsor's or maker's mark, the second is usually the sterling mark, the third is the Assay Office (and this will vary according to which Assay Office tested the article), and the fourth is the date letter mark, indicating the year of assay, as this is changed annually and varies according to the assay town. The shape of the shields and the type of alphabet are all vital, as are any distinguishing dots, crowns etc. Component parts should carry some marks but only one complete set per item.

Sponsor or   Sterling   Assay Office   Date letter
maker's mark

Sterling silver standard
Leopard's head mark (1300 to present day), crowned leopard's head (1478-1821). Lion passant 1544-1697 and 1720 to present day (92.5 per cent silver) if supported by Assay Office mark.

Britannia silver standard
Figure of Britannia used from 1697 to the present day, replaced sterling compulsorily from 1697-1720, thereafter optional. Britannia mark used in conjunction with the Lion's head erased (torn off at the neck) until 1975, therafter Britannia only. Assay Offices other than London have their town mark in addition. From 1784-1890 an extra, temporary mark was used, which was the **duty mark**, the mark was the monarch's head, so during this period five marks will be found on a piece of London silver, and six on most Provincial silver.

Gold
Marked in the same way as sterling standard until 18ct was introduced in 1798. Other lower carats were introduced from mid 19th century. The shape of the date letter shield can differ from silver although the letter is the same.

Platinum
Marks were introduced in 1975. Similar marks to gold and silver except that the standard mark is an orb surmounted by a cross within a pentagon.

Commemorative Mark
For the year of the Silver Jubilee (1934-5) of King George V and Queen Mary, the Coronation (1952-3) and Silver Jubilee (1977) of Queen Elizabeth II, an extra optional mark was introduced, showing the sovereign's head.

Foreign plate
From 1842 all imported plate sold had to be submitted for assay and marking. From 1867 to 1904 an extra mark of F in an oval punch was required to be struck. From 1904 distinct import marks were introduced, (a square punch being used for gold, an oval punch for silver), numerical punches were introduced for standards, and the current date letter was also struck.

PEWTER

Touch mark   the primary mark which gives the name of the pewterer. Of many shapes, styles and designs

Hallmarks   usually four small punched marks, the use of which brought forth protests from the Goldsmiths, which infer neither date, town or quality but are the choice of an individual pewterer and are an extra means of determining his or her identity. First used about 1635

Rose and crown   used from at least 1566 as a quality mark on pewter in Britain. It is used on the Continent as a touch mark

Crowned X   believed to be a quality mark, signifying extraordinary or hard pewter alloy, ie an alloy containing more antimony than usual

METAL
Decoration

DECORATION
A great variety of decorative forms appear on metal items

13th and 14th century stamped tendril ornament

17th and 18th century wrought iron waterleaf

17th and 18th century repoussé sheet iron acanthus

18th century cast iron medallion

Twist

Fish tail

Ribbon end

Ribbon end scroll

Scrolls

Rolled nib

Clip collars

Open scarf collar

Astragal collar

Flat nib or half-penny snub

Fiddlehead

Solid barrel or bolt end

THUMBPIECES

Ramshorn or
Corkscrew

Volute

Scroll

Moulded

Chair

Twin lobe

Open

Pierced

Pomegranate

Bud

Hammerhead

Embryo shell

Bifurcated leaf

Bifurcated

FINIALS OR TERMINALS
at the base of handles

Rat tail

Fish tail

Heel

Spade

Ball

Attention

Shield

Leaf

Scroll

METAL
Fixtures

HINGES

The earliest metal hinges in Norman times recall Viking designs, being usually crescent-shaped with snake-head, tendril or flower terminals. By the 12th century hinges had become more geometrical. The greatest period for metalwork decoration was the 13th century when scrollwork was widely used, before a decline in the quality of blacksmiths' work in the 14th century.

Like handles, hinges are unreliable for dating purposes, since all styles have been copied throughout the centuries.

Decorative strap-hinges
Horizontal straps with diverging channelled scrolled stems and leaves

17th century wrought-iron **Strap-hinge** with stamped decoration on the fleur-de-lys finial

Strap-hinge with incised chevron decoration and fleur-de-lys finial

Gudgeon-hook smithed to a wrought iron lug, over which the eye of the strap-hinge sometimes passed

Pin hung **hook-and-band hinge**, the eye (formed by the band return) passing over a pin

T-hinge

16th and 17th century **butterfly hinges**

16th and 17th century
Cock's head hinge

17th century **H-hinge** or 20th century **Parliament hinge** plain in 18th century

Butt hinge in use from c1680

METAL

KEYS AND LOCKS

Keys made before 1850 usually have bits filed on the front; after 1850 they are filed on the bottom edge

Bow
Shank
Bit

14th century **key** with simple bow, plain shank and thin bit with parallel

Late 17th and 18th century **key** with pierced bow

18th century **cabinet key**

Late 18th century **key** for Tumbler bit latch

19th century **cabinet key**

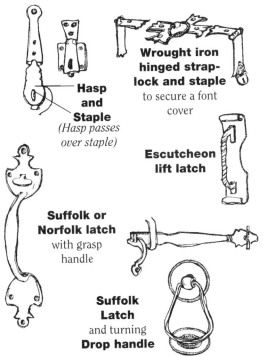

Hasp and Staple
(Hasp passes over staple)

Wrought iron hinged strap-lock and staple to secure a font cover

Escutcheon lift latch

Old Stock Lock and latch with heavy wood casing containing bolt operated by key

Suffolk or Norfolk latch with grasp handle

Suffolk Latch and turning **Drop handle**

16th century **iron lock-plate**

Hatchet-shaped latch with Tumbler bit latch lock

Holdback catch for gates

Keep *(slot into which a bolt is shot)*

107

METAL
Fixtures

HANDLES AND KEY ESCUTCHEONS

Although some handle shapes are typical of a particular period, all have been much copied at different times. Keyholes on English furniture are generally rounded at the base until the 18th century.

1 Square iron lock-plate with trefoil corners 14th, 15th and 16th centuries
2 Iron stirrup with cruciform backplate 16th and 17th centuries
3 Iron loop-drop twist with round backplate 16th and 17th centuries
4 Iron heart-shaped loop-drop on a shaped key escutcheon 16th and 17th centuries
5 Iron ring or Dutch drop (1690-1710)
6 Cast brass pear-drop on circular moulded backplate c1700
7 Split tail or axe-drop on hexafoil backplate early 18th century
8 Acorn drop c1700
9 Tangs and loop on engraved and shaped backplate early 18th century
10 Shield-shaped key escutcheon, often engraved, early 18th century
11 Bail handle passing through cast knobs on solid backplate c1710
12 Bail handle passing through cast knobs on cutaway backplate c1730
13 Bail handle passing through cast knobs on pierced backplate c1750
14 1740-70
15 Dutch drop from 1750
16 Swan-necked loop from two circular moulded backplates from 1750 and much used in the 19th century
17 Mid 18th century Chinoiserie with geometric piercing
18 Rococo with two separate plates for handle sockets and acanthus decoration (decoration sometimes asymmetrical) from c1750. Earlier examples have a single backplate
19 From 1770
20 Relief-stamped oval backplate with plain loop handle passing through two knobs from c1770
21 Circular relief-stamped handle on circular moulded backplate from c1770
22 Lion mask with ring 1790-1820
23 Relief-stamped swan-necked handle attached to oval rose-stamped backplates
24 Beaded circular loop attached to stamped circular backplate c1820
25 Sunken or recessed handle often found on military or travelling chests c1820
26 Art nouveau fixed protruding loop c1900

NAIL AND SCREWS

Tapering metal screws were first introduced in the late 17th century and were hand-filed with irregular threads. Lathe-turned screws appeared in the late 18th century and machine-made screws in the mid 19th century.

pre 1850

post 1850 long shank screw

post 1850 wire nail

17th and 18th century hand-made clout nails

pre 1850 short shank screw

post 1850 oval nail

post 1850

1

2

3

4

5

6

7

8

9

10

11

12

13

14

15

16

17

18

19

20

21

22

23

24

25

26

METAL
Religious Objects

BAPTISM, HOLY WATER, OIL AND INCENSE

Portable font
Cercelée cross iron finial on lid
Oak body with metal lift-out bowl
Hand-forged wrought iron cruciform stand
on oak plinth with chamfered edges

Silver stoup or Holy Water basin
*(usually near the entrance to the church
and more often of stone)*
Backplate of lozenge-shaped cartouche
form with strapwork, repoussé and
hammered decoration, with Sacred
Monogram IHS in plain roman capitals
superimposed on a Latin cross on a central
medallion
Waterleaf decorated bombe basin stepped at
base
Pendant ball and steeple finial

Silver asperges bucket
Tubular lobed bail or swing handle
Moulded floriated double-curved rim
Vase shaped body with chased decoration of
a cupid head and festoons
Collet *(collar)* at junction of body and foot
High domed foot with turned over edge and
matted and scrolled decoration

Asperges or holy water sprinkler
with perforated ball finial and baluster stem
of silver, attached to oak handle with silver
baluster knop

Aspergillum
brush with short handle

Chrismatory
containing set of Holy Oil Stocks
I Oleum Infirmorum (for the sick)
B Oleum Catechumenorum (for Baptism)
C Chrism (for Confirmation and
   Consecration)

Baptismal shell
with shaped silver handle on which is an
engraved Maltese cross

Stem-struck strainer spoon
of Old English pattern c1730 with elliptical
bowl and name of church engraved in script
on handle

Incense dish of boat shape c1742
edged with roll moulding, on baluster stem
above high circular foot stepped at base
Double lid, hinged amidship, with ends of flaps
secured by cast scrolled clasps projecting from
bulwark

Censer or Thurible
Finial encased in a cresting of loops, through
which run three chains rising from attachments
on the base. Domed and stepped cover with
lobed rim, decorated with double roll
mouldings, the dome with pierced dormers
Lobed hexagonal body with everted edge
A roundel applied to each lobe, cusped inside
with a spoke pattern ending in trefoils
Hexagonal foot with double roll edge, each facet
being pierced with a hole for attachments, now
missing. Thumbpiece attached to a trefoil plate

METAL
Religious Objects
BELLS

Bells are hung in the **Bell Chamber**, usually high in the tower or spire of the church. The bells are rung from the **Ringing Chamber** and between them is a **Dead Chamber** or (if it contains a clock) the **Clock Chamber**. In the late 19th century, the Rev Ellacombe introduced a pulley system for bell chimes which is often found and is known as the **Ellacombe Chiming System**.

Bells frequently have names, the majority feminine, but some male, like Great Tom of Oxford or Big Ben. They are stamped with foundry marks and may carry other inscriptions. The character of the lettering and the foundry marks upon old bells are valuable in determining date, although the same stamps were used for centuries and sometimes more than one foundry used the same stamp simultaneously.

Important bells may be listed for preservation by the diocese and their detailed history is often included in descriptive leaflets of the church.

Principal English Bellfoundries

1424-1513	Brasyers of Norwich, Norfolk
1506-1616	Newcombes of Leicester
1518-1709	Knights of Reading
1539-1741	Oldfields of Nottingham
1570-today	The Whitechapel Bell Foundry Ltd, London (incorporating Mot; Bartlet; Phelps; Lester; Pack; Mears; Mears & Stainbank)
1584-1697	Purdues of Somerset
1590-1682	Cliburys of Wellington, Shropshire
1610-1823	Penningtons of Devon and Cornwall
1631-1782	Bagleys of Chacombe, Northamptonshire
1635-1726	Chandlers of Drayton Parslow, Buckinghamshire
1652-1731	Smiths of York
1684-1830	Rudhalls of Gloucester
1698-1814	Bilbies of Chewstoke, Somerset
1788-1809/1853-1918	John Warner & Sons, London
1800-today	John Taylor & Co (Bellfounders) Ltd, Loughborough, Leicestershire

Always ask a trained ringer to lower the bell for examination and do not touch a bell set upside down or pull a rope attached to one
For each bell take note of the name or number
the note
the weight
the inscription
the likely date
the bellfounder
the diameter of the mouth
the presence of cannons and argent
the condition
(cracked or sound)
and if rehung and by whom

Argent — Head
Canons — Crown
— Shoulder
Inscription band
Moulding
Wires — Waist
— Soundbow
— Lip

112

COMMUNION OR EUCHARIST: Cups

The Communion Wine

Before the Reformation, the cup at the centre of the Eucharist was known as a **chalice**; after about 1525 it was known as a **communion cup**, but the term chalice came back into common usage towards the end of the 18th century and for 19th and 20th century cups influenced by pre-Reformation designs.

The most ornate medieval chalices are about 17cm high and set with **cabochons,** whereas similar 19th century examples are larger and mounted with faceted jewels.

12th and 13th century Norman style chalice

Wide shallow bowl with moulded rim, sometimes shallower than illustrated and with everted rim
Cylindrical stem, often quite plain
Spherical knot, either lobed, wrythen, plain or pierced
Circular foot with engraved or raised ornament *(other examples often have stamped beading on the edge)*

Font cup c1510

Font-shaped bowl on sturdy trumpet stem with narrow cabled collet at junction of bowl and stem
Bowl annulated by a band with raised inscription in plain roman capitals, *COMMUNION CUP,* the words separated by tied scrolls on a pounced ground, probably added in the 17th century

Early 16th century pre-Reformation Tudor chalice

Deep bowl with everted rim, set in star-shaped calyx *(cup-like cavity)*
Hexagonal stem with vertical bands of rope moulding at each angle
Gothic knot with six lozenge bosses, each with a tracery motif on red or green enamel on the facets, amidst intervening lobes
Hexagonal lobed foot with saints in cusped niches engraved on the panels, one panel bearing an engraved crucifix

METAL
Religious Objects

Tudor communion cup c1574
Deep bucket-shaped bowl, annulated with band of strapwork and moresques, resting on a compressed hemispherical knot above a wide flange

Foot and base trumpet shaped, with stamped egg and dart moulding on edge

Tudor communion cup c1576
Deep beaker-shaped bowl with everted rim decorated with strapwork arabesque
Lozenge decorated collet joins bowl and spool stem with lozenge ornament at lower edge
Central compressed knot
Domed and stepped circular foot, the lower edge ornamented as on stem, the base encircled with gadrooning

Communion cup c1600
Deep conical bowl engraved with IHS across the stem of a cross, within a sunburst
Baluster stem
High circular foot stepped at base with ring moulding

Communion cup c1686
Deep beaker-shaped bowl with everted rim engraved with armorials on a lozenge, contained within foliate ornament of two crossed branches of laurel tied below with a ribbon. Trumpet-shaped stem with narrow central flange
Shallow stepped and domed circular foot
Inscriptions at this period usually in English in lettering similar to that used on contemporary monuments

Mid 18th century communion cup
Goblet-shaped bowl annulated with applied moulding above which is an engraved IHS within a sunburst and below inverted rays
Trumpet-shaped stem with compressed moulded knot two-thirds of the way up and engraved putti at base
Domed and stepped foot with rayed decoration

Late 18th century communion cup
Ogee-shaped bowl encircled near top with raised foliate ornament and festoons of flowers and foliage
Fluted calyx reaching halfway up the bowl
Baluster stem with spiral gadrooning
Foliated collet joining the stem to the high domed fluted foot on a spreading base which is encircled with raised acanthus leaves

Mid 19th century chalice
Hemispherical bowl annulated with lines of niello enclosing an inscription in 19th century lombardic lettering. Small cast and applied calyx of fleurs-de-lys
Cylindrical stem with stepped mouldings and vertical wires and pellets on a niello ground
Gadroons and foliated mouldings decorate the knot
Filigree scrolls on the collet. Conical foot divided into six panels by rope mouldings each containing an applied roundel with representations of the Evangelists, Agnus Dei and a Greek cross
Stepped circular edge

19th century chalice inspired by Norman style
Plain conical bowl set in an arcaded calyx, with filigree decorated architrave and spandrels, the pillars set with cabuchons. Cylindrical stem annulated with mouldings above and below the angular knot which is decorated with filigree scrolling and eight stone bosses. High circular flaring foot with an inverted filigree arcade, as in the calyx, stepped and moulded edge to base, with a band of filigree ornament

METAL
Religious Objects

20th century chalice
Double cone or egg-timer shape, the bowl
shallower than the base
Lower third of bowl and whole stem base
decorated with hammered abstract geometrical
designs

Collets

Lozenge
Boss

Gothic
Knot/Knop

Billet decoration
on Riser

Chalice showing an amalgamation of decorative details from two silver gilt
chalices of 1525 and 1527

Hemispherical bowl annulated with a band inscribed in gothic lettering on a hatched
ground *CALICEM • SALUTARIS • ACCIPIAM • ET • NOMEN • DOMINI • INVOCABO*
Hexagonal collet of stepped moulding below the bowl and above the knot.
Hexagonal stem, rising from a balustrade with pinnacles at the angles, displaying
panels of pierced quatrefoil tracery within cabling, interrupted by a large lobed
Gothic knot with six projecting lozenge bosses embellished with raised human
masks on the facets.
The panels of the high hexagonal foot are decorated in two stages, the upper with
feathering, the lower with plain lettering on a hatched ground (indecipherable).
One bell-shaped panel, protruding from the others, is engraved with a crucifix, the
rim of the bell curving onto the bottom step of a circular stepped flange.
Wavy-edged hexagonal stepped base with stamped vertical billet decoration on the riser.

THE SACRAMENT

Ciborium   covered receptacle for storing the consecrated Hosts, distinguishable from cup or chalice, when found without the cover, by rim or ledge **(bezel)** on which the cover rests

Monstrance decorative container for Sacrament to be displayed to worshippers

Paten   plate on which the Sacrament is served during Eucharist

Pyx   box for carrying the Sacrament to the sick

Salver   plate, larger than paten, for serving Sacrament during Eucharist

Tabernacle decorative container for the ciborium or wafer box (see page 11)

Tazza   wine cup with shallow circular bowl mounted on foot, often confused with patens or salvers

Wafer box   box for storing the wafers

Ciborium
Baluster finial supporting a Patonce cross set with a white sapphire

Slightly domed and stepped cover, *(which should be hallmarked)*

Shaped hemispherical bowl with bezel to support the cover

Hexagonal collet at junction of bowl and hexagonal stem

Stepped collet above and below a Wrythen pierced Gothic knot bearing six lozenge bosses with raised foliate ornament set with sapphire centres

Stepped collet at junction of stem and hexagonal incurving foot
Edge engraved with band of reeding
Six pierced trefoil toes

METAL
Religious Objects

THE SACRAMENT: Patens

Normally a simple flat decorated plate, the paten can have a foot and stem (**standing patens**) and certain 17th century covered patens are furnished with spool feet and covers and resemble ciboria. The covers of such standing patens are often an inverted copy of the base, known as **paten lids**, and were used in the 16th century to double as covers for the communion cup. The base of a paten is often decorated with a button bearing the Sacred Monogram or the name of the church in a roundel.

12th-14th century paten

Circular with double depression. Band contained within the moulded rim circumscribed in plain lombardic uncials on a hatched ground + *CALICEM SALUTARIS ACCIPIAM ET NOMEN DOMINI INVOCABO,* a cross at the beginning and lozenge devices between each word Domed centre engraved with Head of Christ set in roundel within an engraved sunburst on a matted ground, all within an embossed sexfoil with spandrels engraved with small sun motifs. On the reverse, Sacred Monogram in Latin form

Standing paten c1576

Bezel to fit communion cup. Spool foot, with button on base. Button engraved horizontally with date in arabic numerals. Reeded outer edge, similar to top Spool finial, outside annulated with a band of strapwork and moresques. Inside of paten lid undecorated with single depression and single reeded border to narrow rim, with protruding bezel

Monstrance

Silver, parcel-gilt and set with carbuncles in the form of a shrine. Glazed crested roundel in the centre front, edged with rope moulding and fleurs-de-lys tracery, to contain the Sacrament. The roundel is supported on a stepped silver plinth with gilt moulding, engraved dog-tooth patterning and set with five carbuncles. On each side, a buttress decorated with tracery and geometric patterns, pinnacled and crocketed, with niches containing two gilt figures of angels holding crowns. Above the roundel, a gabled silver roof, with dormers, engraved with a sexfoil foliated device, set with carbuncles and with gilt cresting A floriated gilt cross with central carbuncle at apex of roof. Shrine rests on hexagonal stem decorated with engraved dog-tooth and other ornament, branching at top into scrolls and crockets and edged horizontally with brattishing. Compressed spherical knot with embossed lobes and six bosses, each framed in swirling crockets and set with a carbuncle. Gilt collet at junction of stem and foot. Hexfoil foot, parcel-gilt, decorated with foliated ornament on matted ground, with carbuncles set in each foil; base with gilt mouldings and engraved decoration

118

Salver c1693 used as a paten

Narrow rim with triple reeded border

Single depression with shallow straight-sided bouge

Slight moulded collet at junction of top and high flaring foot which is edged with ovolo decoration and stands on a narrow flanged base. Incised armorials in centre of well. Marks are: London assay 1693; maker's mark PM within quatrefoil. All marks are in the well except that of the lion passant which is on the underside of the flange. Underneath the salver is incised 1713.

Patens and salvers are often confused with **tazzas** *which are deeper bodied wine cups.*

Plate paten

Broad rimmed plate with engraved patée cross on rim

Inscription engraved in roman capitals on back of rim

Dish paten

Saucer dish with shallow foot-rim

Hammered decoration covering inside

Circle within triangle

Edge

Triquetra

Rim

Well

Stepped depression

Interwoven circles

Alms dish

(usually large plate of base metal over 30cm diameter)

Circular silver alms dish with enamelled decoration (40.5cm diameter), with moulded patterned edge to panelled rim

Three medallions rise from bosses in stepped depression of the dish, containing embossed representations of The Holy Trinity (triquetra; circle within triangle; interwoven circles, see page 25) framed by enamelled wing forms arching back to and framing silver reliefs of sailing ships on rim

In the centre the Sacred Monogram IHS in plain roman capitals in a blue enamelled roundel within pink and white coiled rope pattern

METAL
Religious Objects

Pyx
(vessel used to carry the Sacrament to the sick, usually a box smaller than a wafer box but found in many forms)

Wafer box
with lift out grid

Altar tabernacle in three stages
Crocketed pinnacle terminating in a foliated finial

Open (to contain monstrance) with buttresses supporting hexagonal canopy, pinnacled and gabled

Square base, each side with crocketed gable; door at front, decorated with raised cross set with crystals
At the intersection Agnus Dei on an enamelled roundel

Hanging tabernacle
with veil

CROSSES

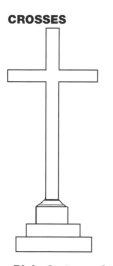

**Plain 3-stepped
Latin Calvary
altar cross**

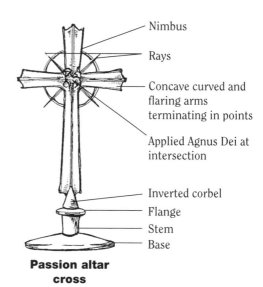

Nimbus

Rays

Concave curved and
flaring arms
terminating in points

Applied Agnus Dei at
intersection

Inverted corbel

Flange

Stem

Base

**Passion altar
cross**

Processional cross Celtic-style

Handwrought brass wheel cross with
repoussé Celtic ornament on the
splayed limbs and wheel or nimbus
Central concave sided lozenge
medallion displaying Sacred Monogram
IHS in plain roman letters on a chased
ground. Spandrels of the nimbus
similarly chased
Compressed and annulated brass knot
and cylindrical stem joins the cross to
the screw-jointed oak stem with brass
ferrule at base

Screw joint

Pectoral cross
incorporating rose and heart
emblems in gold and enamel

Brass ferrule

121

METAL
Religious Objects

Hanging Crucifix
with integral Corpus Christi and scroll of
gun metal with INRI in roman capitals

Wall or hanging cross
deeply modelled and textured
in aluminium alloy with
bright chromium plated
finish
Centre of coloured faceted
slab glass set in epoxy resin
Rustic shape with silhouette

Fimbriated pommée Altar Cross
with projecting fleurs-de-lys at the angles of
the arms forming an openwork nimbus
A Chi Rho in a roundel at the intersection
The four terminals embellished with three
fleurs-de-lys crockets, each set with a
jewel. Two pairs of smaller fleurs-de-lys
crockets adorn the lower arm
An inverted corbel above a stepped flange
attaches the shaft supporting the cross to a
cylindrical stem which is stepped at the base
The high domed circular foot has a band of
trefoil decoration between annulations on the
dome. The vertical edge of the foot has a
moulded flanged base

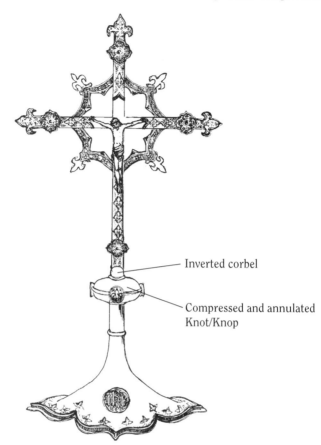

Inverted corbel

Compressed and annulated
Knot/Knop

METAL

Mid-19th century Crucifix

The arms are engraved with fleurs-de-lys in diaper pattern. To each arm is attached a
quatrefoil edged with roll moulding, engraved with foliage on a matted ground, set with
a single amethyst. The three upper arms terminate in fleurs-de-lys with roll mouldings and
engraved foliage centres. The intersection of the arms, outlined with gables of roll
moulding but otherwise left plain as a background to the head and arms of Christ, is
surrounded by an octagon, cusped on its inner side, concave on its outer and crested on the
four exposed angles with fleurs-de-lys, the width filled with a band of dog-tooth ornament
between roll mouldings on a hatched ground *(for figure see page 53)*.

An inverted corbel is placed at the junction of the cross and the knot of the annulated
cylindrical stem. The compressed and annulated spherical knot has four bosses
bearing applied roundels of fleurs-de-lys on blue enamel.

The high tapering foot is engraved with the Sacred Monogram IHS, on a hatched ground
within a roundel, a cursive band of engraved trefoils follows the wavy four-lobed edge.

An engraved band of hatching occupies the space between the edge of the foot and the base.
The frame of the cross is of wood cased on the front in plates of base metal, the base
is of electroplated base metal and the figure of Christ is electrogilt.

METAL
Religious Objects

LECTERNS

Lecterns became a feature of post-Reformation churches, usually very austere and made up of an amalgamation of different decorative parts. From the beginning of the 19th century lecterns became more simple. **Book stands** are particularly used to support the priest's **missal** during services.

Brass lectern c1683

Book desk in form of an eagle with outstretched wings flanked by single bracket candle holders with glass tulip- shaped shades, standing on a sphere which is supported on a flaring concave section above various bands of moulding including some raised leaf work
Baluster stem with a stepped circular base
Cylindrical section springing from stepped moulding above the high-domed lectern base resting on four lion sejant feet

Late 19th century brass lectern

Double desk with gable ends pierced with cusped circular openings and band of cresting across top
Cylindrical stem decorated with rings of red and blue inlaid mastic with formalised leaf forms supporting the desk
Central compressed spherical knot with attached band with knobbed decoration, scalloped edges and trefoil collets above and below
Trefoil collet at junction of stem and base
Conical base which is decorated with pierced sexfoils and annulations of red and blue inlaid mastic
Stands on four red painted paw feet (which have been restored) protruding from the cusped edge

Pedestal type missal or book stand
in highly polished brass with revolving bookplate embellished with pierced quatrefoils within roundels in the corners, and a central roundel with Sacred Monogram IHS in Latin form on punched ground
Rope moulded edge to bookplate, screwjoint and trumpet base

METAL

Ledger type missal or book stand
with cast scrolled and foliated end panels and scalloped edge to bookplate ledge

Pulpit desk
with quatrefoil decoration in centre and a scalloped ledge
Adjustable stem (by use of key) attached to inside of pulpit drum by clips to square bracket plates with trefoil corners

METAL
Religious Objects
PROCESSIONAL

Finial

Collet

Ferrule

Shaft

Hinged retaining clip

Ferrule
or
shoe

Candle extinguisher and taper holder
Brass cone-shaped extinguisher with rolled edge and patée cross finial. Bent cylindrical taper holder attached by brass ferrule to oak stem

Pax
(tablet with projecting carrying handle behind, decorated on front with rood or sacred symbol)

Church Warden's wand (usually screw jointed and with various finials)

Verger's wand *(similar to Church Warden's but shorter)*

Morse
(badge sewn or pinned to band joining sides of cope, sometimes embroidered but usually metal)
Holy Trinity in basse-taille enamel (see page 101) on silver with pierced gold outer rim

Pastoral staff or crozier
Silver gilt, decorated with enamels and semi-precious stones
Hexagonal crook, imbricated and set with stones, terminating in serpent's head with forked tongue. The curve is connected to the stem by a foliated ornament
Central figures of Christ (standing) charging St Peter (seated) on an enamelled ground
Four marks above niches, maker's mark, sterling standard, Assay Office and date
Flanking the stem are two tiers of niches, separated by pinnacled buttresses, occupied by figures of saints and bishops under foliated canopies; upper tier is surmounted by three more figures standing against alternate facets of the hexagonal stem
Plinth of the lower tier of niches is set on a foliated boss rising, by a concave stem, from a knot decorated with swirling gadroons
A shield, bearing the arms of the See, is set on the ferrule of the oak staff

GATES AND RAILINGS

Overthrow
Cornice
Top rail
Top rail
Lockrail
Dograil
Bottom rail

17th century wrought iron gates (pair)

Overthrow of two large bifurcated S scrolls, passing through central collar and decorated with small scrolls including fiddle head, flat penny nibs and pair of well placed waterleaves

Frieze of strapwork between two square section rails below cornice

Plain square section top rail

Double lockrail with strapwork frieze

Plain square section bottom rail with dograil of arrowheads

In each gate there are four square section verticals, between unadorned stiles, the verticals being mortised, tenoned and welded through the horizontals

16th century wrought iron tomb railing

Fleur-de-lys alternating with spiked finials to the uprights which change to flat section above the top rail

Main verticals with ball and steeple finials, ornamented with double bar twist below the top rail

METAL
Practical Objects

LIGHTING

Candlesticks

17th century pewter candlestick
Bell shaped

17th century brass candlestick
Vertical slot in cylindrical stem with protruding candle ejector
Drip pan in centre of stem
Wide spreading base

Late 17th century silver or gilt Baroque style candlestick
Gadrooned drip pan and pricket
Baluster stem shaped and ornamented
Scrolled tripod base surmounted by putti

Classical silver candlestick c1675
Fluted and reeded column of Doric form with broad platform at base
High waisted plinth
Large square stepped and domed foot

Early 18th century silver or brass candlestick
Steel rod ejector in base
Reel-shaped sconce on distinct neck
Shouldered baluster stem with knots
Moulded and depressed polygonal foot

Neo-classical style silver or brass late 18th century candlestick
Tapering fluted stem
High trumpet-shaped foot
Bell shaped leaf - decorated sconce with separate nozzle

METAL

METAL

Nozzle and drip pan scalloped, with deep indentations between each pair of scallops, annulated with two pairs of incised rings

Drip Pan
Cylindrical stem with three knots, the upper one gem set and chased with zigzag ornament, the lower little more than a flange

Knot

Stem between them annulated by double rows of incised rings enclosing a zigzag pattern

Flange

Large compressed central knot, chased and decorated with bead mouldings and with stones as bosses

Stem decorated as above, with rings and zigzag pattern

Moulded collets
High conical foot
Panels formed of chased lines with stones set in high collets

Pierced cusped openings alternating with pierced roundels

19th century altar copper gilt candlestick
set with semi-precious stones

METAL
Practical Objects

METAL (vertical sidebar)

Five-branch candelabrum

Brass flat-scrolled branches with ivy leaf repoussé
ornament springing from top of cylindrical stem,
holding shallow saucer-shaped drip pans with
scalloped cresting and annulated cylindrical nozzles
Central fifth socket at top of reeded rod with scrolling
brackets
Polychrome imbricated iron stem with brass terminal
ferrule, passing through collar of base and joined, by a
brass knot, at top to a brass cylindrical stem
Wrought iron tripod base formed of broken scrolled
legs with ribbon ends, united by wide incurving collar
with bolt-end terminals

Highly polished brass processional torch or bier light

(135cm h to pan)
Incurving four sided
tapering drip pan with
plain cylindrical socket
Cylindrical stem with
two compressed and
stepped knots
Removable four sided
incurving and tapering
base on four bun feet

Flowerstand

(adapted from torchere)
Disc top with embattled gallery
Twist stem joined by spindle collet
to rectangular section supported by
scrolled cruciform bracket feet
united to stem by clip collars in
three places

16th century wrought iron bracket of prickets, attached to wall and pivoted

Two horizontal bars, connected by spiral
uprights, forming five open panels with
spike at midpoint of base of each as support
for candle which passes through ring in
upper bar, crested with alternating fleurs-
de-lys and cocks

METAL

Branch candelabrum

**Pyramid style candelabrum
with hexagon base**

Rushlight holder

**Slant style candelabrum
with round base**

Strap sconce

Delta branch candelabrum

**Seven branch Jerusalem
candlestick or menorah**

14th century wrought iron **herse** *(top)*
erected around or over tombs for their
protection with fleur-de-lys decorated
candle prickets

METAL
Practical Objects

Votive stand
Stove-enamel finish, 33 lights, slide-out tray

Votive stand
Wrought iron, 16 lights, aluminium drip pans with brass pickets

Either of these stands may be fitted with sanctum lights or glasses

Hanging lights

Lanterns and chandeliers in churches were used to supplement candlesticks from around 1600, first plain English chandeliers and later in the century, more ornate Dutch examples.

The commonest shape of 17th century chandelier has drooping branches hooked into rings in the balusters or into trays pierced with holes. The branches are mostly circular in section and of two opposed curves with moulding at the join, so that the inner end forms an open spiral and the outer end is everted. The finial at the top was often highly decorative and different provincial centres had their own characteristic finials.

During the 18th century, the arms became shorter, drooped less and were fitted to the circumference of a flatter central sphere. The branches themselves were more elaborate, often hexagonal or octagonal in section and covered with scrolling. The spaces between the branches and tiers were filled with ornament, usually gadrooning and the most popular finial was a flame. Dutch chandeliers in the 18th century had no finials or ornament and the branches were attached to hollow trays by tenons and pins, rather than hooks. Chandeliers made from 1600 to 1900 have solid arms whereas 20th century chandeliers have hollow arms to take the electrical wiring.

METAL

Tiers of curving branches, usually two or three

Brass chandelier of mixed date

Top finial

London dove finial
(Bristol dove has closed wings and no feathers on body)

Shaft of ball and baluster turnings (hollow and held together by an iron hanging rod)

Pendant finial

Oil lamp

with clear glass chimney and opaque china hemispherical shade
Brass body fitting into an annulated iron girdle to which are attached three wrought iron broken-scrolled brackets suspended from iron link chains

METAL
Practical Objects

Wrought iron corona lucis

Hanging by chains from circlet crested
with fleurs-de-lys
Bowl drip pans under eight candle
sockets similarly ornamented and
attached to outer side of coronet by
twist stems with pendant turnip-shaped
finials, the joins hidden by an applied
fleur-de-lys decorated shields, painted
red and gold
Rims of annulated coronet decorated
with fleurs-de-lys

Sanctuary lamp

Highly polished brass with cast and
finely modelled Dolphin arms attached
by their tails to a ball and baluster
pendant finial of the drip pan, by their
snouts to the socket in which an eight
day type ruby glass cylindrical funnel
with everted lip rests, and by their
dorsal fins to three chains hanging
from a brass circlet surmounted with a
ring similar to that at the base of the
pendant finial

*Describe the shape and ornament of every part and the way the light is fitted
together. For chandeliers, record the number of tiers, the number of branches
in each tier and the finials*

Bracket Lights

Brass candle sconce

Cartouche-shaped sconce with repoussé decoration and central uninscribed cartouche, lower part reeded and fluted
Simple knotted s-shaped arm of round section springing from a floriated boss at the base of the sconce, holding plain saucer-shaped drip pan with annulated cylindrical nozzle moulded at rim

Brass candle bracket

Horizontal rod of square section interrupted by twists, emerging from fleurette on backplate, supported above and below by inward scrolling waterleaf brackets, terminating in trefoil
Floral collar near terminal is threaded with stem of urn-shaped socket

19th century wrought iron hexagonal porch lantern

Baluster finial with attached ring
Double domed cover with ogee ribs and scrolled-over lower edge, pierced panels with whorls (lower dome) and lozenges (upper dome)
Band with rectangular piercing between domes
Tapering glazed panels with iron traceried glazing bars in heads fixed to scrolled-over crested upper rail with band of pierced arcading between scroll and scrolled-over lower edge of cover
Pendant finial of scrolled brackets radiating from centre to plain moulded outside edges of bottom rail of glazed panels

METAL

METAL
Practical Objects

Brass bracket gasolier
Band of floral engraving on the globe which sits in a trefoil crested socket with acorn pendant finial
Waterleaf decorated scrolled arm with cast brass fleurette inner terminal to the scroll end near wall plate
Scroll end linked to waterleaf stem

Sanctuary bracket lamp
Bright polished chromium plate with glass funnel nestling in calyx above disc set on flaring reeded stem sitting in a collar at the end of a shaped triangular wall bracket

Processional torch
Chromium plated brass torch on teak stem with clear glass cylindrical funnel. A handle-grip of textured brass to prevent it slipping through collar of wall mounted bracket

TANKARDS, FLAGONS AND JUGS

Beaker shaped, lipped vessel without a handle or a stem
Cup term applied in old documents to any form of drinking vessel
Flagon large vessel from which other vessels are filled
Mug cylindrical drinking vessel without lid
Tankard drinking vessel with handle and hinged lid

Finial
Cover
Thumbpiece
Shaped lip
Body
Handle
Handle terminal or finial
Stem
Foot
Edge of foot
Flagon

Girdle
Base
Font ewer
(32cm h or more)

Flagon
glass with silver mounts

Cruet
glass with silver mounts

Viaticum
(for carrying communion to the sick)

Lip

Beaker

Lavabo jug and bowl
Body of bowl slightly tucked at base above applied spreading gadrooned foot

137

METAL

Silver flagon c1630
Flat cap lid with moulded thumbpiece
pierced with heart motif
Two marks only (assay and date) inside lid
Tall cylindrical body with boldly cast lip,
engraved on front with armorials and
inscription in contemporary script
Three marks by handle (sterling, assay
and date)
Hollow scroll handle of tapering form with
simple shield-shaped finial
Spreading skirt foot with moulded band above
Stepped and moulded edge to base

James I pewter flagon c1610
with knopped lid; ridged, erect thumbpiece
Plain strap handle. Slightly tapering body with
moulded foot. The bottom of the drum of the
flagon is curved and does not touch the surface
on which the flagon stands, the moulded foot
performing that function
*(In a few cases a flat base has been fixed across
the bottom of the foot)*

Spire pewter flagon c1720-1800
Knopped and domed cover
Tapering body
Curved solid thumbpiece
S-shaped handle
Domed foot
Double fillet just above base

Britannia metal (pewter) flagon c1790-1900
Domed lid
Palmate thumbpiece
Double-scrolled handle with fishtail finial
Large spout
Slightly tapering drum
Several fillets near gently curving
flange foot

19th century flagon with pear-shaped ruby glass body and electrogilt mounts

High domed mount attached to hinged cover (with trefoil thumbpiece) decorated with row of tracery edged with rope moulding and cresting of trefoils surrounding wire-work nest supporting Pelican in her Piety. Plain lip, triangular in section projecting from band of engraved vine ornament. Scroll handle with mouchette tracery in roundel and bifurcated terminal.

Upper mount annulated with roll moulding and pendant cut-card fleurs-de-lys below frieze of quatrefoil tracery surmounted by inscription CHRIST SO LOVED US in plain roman capitals enclosed by roll mouldings on hatched ground.

Engraved metal roundel edged with cut-card trefoils enclosing the Sacred Monogram IHS on front of pear-shaped ruby glass body between mounts which encase upper and lower parts. Lower mount annulated with roll moulding surmounted by cut-card fleurs-de-lys.

High quatrefoil foot with moulded edge engraved with crosses within roundels, hatched as for inscription.

**Hourglass
stands**

Dog tongs

**17th century
swordrest**

COINS AND MEDALS

Both the side with the monarch's head (**obverse**) and the decorative side
(**reverse**) are of interest and can be recorded with a rubbing.

JEWELLERY

Jewels set in 19th and 20th century church plate are likely to be facetted whereas
earlier gems are usually cabochon.

Cabochon	stone of rounded natural form, polished but not cut
Cameo	two layers of glass, the top layer cut in relief to reveal the underlayer
Carbuncle	bright red stone
Facet	one side of cut gem
Filigree	gold or silver wire or pellets applied to gold or silver base in ornamental patterns
Girandole	openwork clasp of alternating ribbon and bow design set with stones
Intaglio	gem with incised design

PAPER
Prints and Paintings

A miscellany of objects in churches may be made of paper or have paper as their chief material. In addition, certain framed objects dealt with under WOOD, for example, **The Roll of Honour**, may in fact appear on paper. **Paintings** are dealt with here though their chief material is most often canvas not paper.

FRAMED OBJECTS

All kinds of framed paper objects will be found in churches, hung on the wall or in drawers. The most interesting features of all framed objects will be the name of the artist, the date of the work, its subject matter and, in the case of maps and architectural drawings, its scale.

Architectural drawings	give vital clues to changes in the church's development; interesting to compare with appearance today
Drawings and watercolours	often of religious scenes, of the church, or local landscape
Certificates	usually framed
List of Vicars	often framed manuscript, or painted on wood or stone
Painting	most likely to be copy of religious work, sometimes well known, in ornate frame which may be interesting, if old
Photographs	the date, the sitter and the photographer may be interesting
Prints	impression in ink on paper, usually framed but may be unframed. Often engravings of contemporary works of art, giving the artist's name alongside the engraver's
Roll of Honour	list of members of parish who fought in World War I 1914-18 and World War II 1939-45, usually framed and glazed and may be illuminated with regimental badges
Stamps	often found amongst faculties and correspondence, most interesting when on envelopes with indication of date
Vignette	small picture without defined borders

PRINTS

Technical terms used in the lettering are usually in Latin or French with abbreviations and contemporary spelling. There are three main recognisable types:

Intaglio	line, steel, stipple engraving; etching; dry point and aquatint
Relief or relievo	woodcuts or wood engravings
Lithographic	printing from stone; resembles drawing with very soft pencil
Laid down	anything pasted on paper
Original engraving	engraved by the artist
Proof	signed by the artist and the engraver
Proof before letters	unsigned, the name of the artist and engraver printed
Lettered proof	title of subject, name of artist, engraver and publisher printed

INSCRIPTIONS

comp	composuit	designed by
del. fig. gez	delineavit, figuravit, dessiné, gezeichnet	drawn by
exc. imp	excudit, impressit	printed by
fac. fec. inc	facet, fecit, incidit, sculpsit	made by
inv	invenit	original artist
pinx. ping	pinxit, pinguit, peint	painted by

Most church documents are now deposited in the county record office, where enquirers can usually view them on request. A series of books, mostly in current use, will, however, be kept in the church, in the church chest, belfry or vestry, or possibly in the rectory.

BOOKS AND PUBLICATIONS FOUND IN CHURCHES

Faculty	authorisation from Diocesan Chancellor (or from 1993, Archdeacon) for alteration or addition to the church. It may give date and names of architect/designer, donor, and materials
Library	many churches have a library of ecclesiastical works
Minute Book	record of meetings of parochial church council (ecclesiastical) not to be confused with parish council (civil)
Missal	earlier name for service book used at Eucharist. If large, for use of priest at altar
Register	record of baptisms, marriages, and burials, sometimes in the same volume
Terrier	record of lands, goods and possessions of parish church
Visitors' Book	record of visitors to the church from outside the parish

Other books found are registers of services, gift books, war memorial books, village histories, bibles, prayer books and other service books; sheet music; descriptive leaflets; parish magazines.

TERMS

Association copy	book associated by ownership or annotation with the author, or with someone connected with the author
Backbone	spine of book
Bands (raised)	ridges on spine caused by the sewing cords, or added (flat) in imitation for decoration
Binding	covering of outside boards of book
Blind tooled	impressions stamped without gold infill
Boards	sides of bound or cased book
Bolts	folds which have to be cut before the pages can be read
Bookplate or **ex libris**	owner's identification label, usually pasted inside front cover; may be early, eg heraldic, or designed by interesting artist
Boss	knob of brass or other metal fastened on boards for protection of binding or for decoration
Call-mark	see **Shelf-mark**
Cartouche	loosely applied to round, oval or decorated labels and bookplates
Case-bound	book cover made completely before being attached
Clasp	hinged catch for holding together the two covers of the book
Colophon	in early printed books, a statement of the printer's name, date and place of publication at the end of the book, later superseded by title page; it may include publisher's imprint or device

PAPER
Books and bookbinding

Deckle	rough natural edge of hand-made paper
Dedication copy	presented by author to person to whom the book is dedicated
Dentelle	border of lacy pattern on inner edge
Doublure	edge of binding turned in and visible, often decorated; can also mean lining of silk, etc replacing endpapers
Dust cover or jacket	protective loose paper cover
Enclosures	any material not part of the book but inserted in it (eg letters, pictures, cuttings)
Endpapers	leaves of plain or ornamental paper added by binder, one half of each (**the paste-down**) being attached to the inside of the cover, and the other (**the flyleaf**) loose
Ex libris	see **Bookplate**
Fillet	tooled line on cover
Finishing	lettering and decoration
Fleuron	flower-shaped device stamped on bindings, often at corners
Flyleaf	see **Endpapers**
Fore-edge	edge opposite spine; **fore-edge paintings** show when the fore-edge is spread out
Format	statement indicative of shape, size and make-up of book (eg octavo, folio etc)
Foxing	freckle-like brownish spots on paper caused by damp
French grooves	deep concave joints between spine and boards
Gauffering	gilt edges decorated with finishing tools
Guards	folded strips of paper sewn or pasted into the back during rebinding
Gutter	adjoining inside margins of page
Head and tail	top and bottom of spine
Headpiece	printed ornament or illustration at head of chapter or section; see also **Vignette**
Headband	in early or fine binding: protective beading worked in silk thread at head and tail; in modern binding: pasted strip glued on for decoration
Headcap	leather at top and tail of spine, drawn out to cover the headband
Hollow-backed	binding method in which spine is attached to a paper tube; see also **Tight-backed**
Horae or Book of Hours	manuscript or printed collection of the monastic day offices and prayers for private use
Inscribed	copy autographed by the author, usually at the request of the owner
Label (skiver)	thin pieces of morocco (even on a calf book) with lettering From 1750 paper labels were applied to paper spines
Limited edition	usually individually numbered, often by hand
Manuscript	book or document written by hand

Marbling	process of colouring endpapers in variegated patterns based on patterns in marble
Mint condition	as good as new
Octavo (8vo)	leaf of paper folded three times, ie into eight, usually between 15 and 25cm high
Panel	rectangle formed of single or multiple fillets, gilt or blind-stamped on boards or between bands on spine
Panel stamp	leather bindings decorated in blind with a large stamping tool
Paperback	book without hard covers; cover may nowadays be synthetic material or glazed paper
Perfect binding	(or **rubber-back** or **glue-back**) book made in **sections** but held together by adhesive
Plate	illustration printed separately and sometimes on different paper from the text
Presentation copy	spontaneous gift of the author, the value lying in the interest of the recipient or his connection with the author
Provenance	pedigree of book's previous ownership
Quarto (4to)	leaf of paper folded twice, ie into four, usually between 25 and 40cm high
Recto	right hand page
Repairs	books may be re-backed, re-joined, re-margined, re-set
Rotulus	book in roll form
Roll-stamp	cylindrical tool cut in relief to repeat its designs in rotation
Rubric	instruction or heading introducing sections of text; (originally a capital letter distinguished by red ink)
Sections	folded sheets of paper, usually of four or eight leaves or multiples thereof, from which the book is made up
Semis	repeating pattern made with small tools (**seme**)
Shelf-mark	group of numbers or letters indicating place on library shelf; may provide clue to original owner
Signature	letter or numeral at foot of page to indicate sequence of sheets; see also **Sections**
Stamped	impressed with gold or left blind
Tailpiece	printed ornament or illustration at end of chapter or book, see also **Vignette**
Tight-backed or fast-backed:	binding method in which spine is attached directly to the back of the sections; see also **Hollow-backed**
Title page	page at beginning giving particulars of title, authorship, date, publisher, place, etc
Tooling	decoration of cover by hand tools
Uncut	edges left uncut by rebinding (not to be confused with bolts)
Verso	left hand page
Vignette	illustration without a border, often used as head or tail piece
Watermark	mark in paper visible when held to light and helpful in dating printing

PAPER

PAPER
Books and bookbinding

Full bound

Half bound

Quarter bound

Three-quarters bound

Headband
Label
Spine
Field
Band
Joint
Board
Tail

Paste-down (or board paper)
Top edge
Fore edge
Free end-paper or fly leaf

Book in slip case

BINDINGS

Armorial	stamped with a coat of arms, possibly added at a later date. Royal arms do not necessarily denote royal ownership, even if the book is dedicated to a royal personage
Calf	smooth, without grain, can be variously treated and coloured
Etruscan	classical decoration of urn, stylized palm leaves, or key decoration
Fanfare style:	
Forel binding	parchment dressed to look like vellum
Irish	paper lozenge label in centre of board
Mosaic	polychrome decoration of binding by use of paint, onlays or inlays
Parchment	usually sheep or goat, prepared for writing or painting
Publishers cloth	apart from paperback, the usual style of commercial binding, introduced in 1823
Rococo	c-shaped curves and shell decoration popular in the late 1770's and 1780's
Russia leather	rich, smooth cowhide, scented, often decorated with blind lozenge pattern
Scots binding	wheel pattern
Signed binding	binder's or designer's name or initials forming part of design
Sombre binding	black leather, tooled in blind, popular 1675-1725
Spanish calf	bold dashes of red and green acid on calf binding
Tree calf	calf binding with sides stained to resemble trees or foliage
Vellum	very fine parchment or calf
Yapp binding	limp leather with overlapping edges (from 19th century bookseller's name)

Red leather binding with silver panels on both covers

Upper cover: Three bands of spiralling ribbon decoration with moulded edges and set with enamels bearing Sacred Monograms on copper (all much worn), descending diagonally from R to L
On top L corner, an enamelled shield with coat of arms (Arg. a cross Gu. in dexter chief a fleur-de-lys Az.) surrounded by rope moulding with fleur-de-lys finials flanking the shield at the top
Raised lobed bosses at top and bottom R corners

Lower cover: Eight inset enamels on copper
In top R corner an enamelled swan with motto below, surrounded by rope moulding
Raised lobed bosses at top and bottom L corners
Brass clasp with roundel of mouchette tracery on upper cover

BIBLES

Every church will have at least one copy of the Bible, it is most likely to be one of the following:

Great Bible 1539 - 1541, seven editions, re-printing ceased 1569
Cranmer's Bible 1540, long preface by Archbishop Cranmer
Breeches Bible 1560, roman type, see Genesis, ch III, v7
Authorised Version 1611
Revised Version 1881, 1884, 1895 (parts)
Two Version edition 1900

Essential information is author, title, place of publication (if other than London) publisher and date. Note the illustrator, format, page height, binding, inscriptions and other marks if the volume is of special interest

Format: (for book) *A N AUTHOR, Title of book, Publisher, Town, Date* **(for article in journal)** *A N AUTHOR, 'Title of article', 'Title of journal' vol xxx, 1976, pages 36-41* **(for information taken from a church leaflet)** *name and location of church, nth edition, 1977*

STONE
Terms

Churches were often the earliest stone buildings in the community. The majority are still stone built, although other materials, such as brick, flint or concrete, have been used where they are common as a local building material or where fashion demands. Decorative features found in stone will be similar in other building materials. Ornamental stonework is often an important aspect of the decoration of a church, so that, although much of the appropriate terminology is strictly architectural *(see ARCHITECTURE)*, identification should be easier by reference to stone features in this chapter. Certain features, including **pulpits, feretories and screens**, are more likely to be wooden than stone in Britain and are therefore treated in the chapter on *WOOD*.

Aumbry — cupboard, usually for the Reserved Sacrament, in north wall of chancel (see page 11)

Chamfer — the narrow surface formed when an angle is cut away obliquely. It may be moulded, concave *(hollow)*, sunk or stopped

Credence — table or shelf near the altar, usually on the south side

Easter sepulchre — canopied recess in north chancel wall, similar to a tomb chest, used to contain the Sacrament or effigy of Christ between Good Friday and Easter Morning. Occasionally of wood

Mensa — stone altar-top incised with five consecration crosses

Pillar piscina — piscina on pillar, freestanding or against wall

Piscina — basin with drain, used for washing sacred vessels, set into wall, sill or floor south of an altar

Sedilia (s. sedile) — seats for clergy, generally on south side of chancel

Squint — aperture pierced through wall to allow view of altar

Stoup — receptacle for holding holy water often in the form of a deeply dished stone set in a niche or on a pillar near a doorway

Stone brackets
for statues or statuettes

Pillar piscina

Corbel

Credence shelf

Mensa

Cresset stone
(Stone with cup-like hollows filled with oil and floating wicks to give light for those performing night duties in church) (rare today)

Aumbry

Bread oven

Squint

Piscina

14th century Easter sepulchre

Canopied recess of three bays with crocketed, pinnacled and cusped ogee arches, above a shelf, resembling a tomb chest with four panels of similar blind arched decoration Adjacent on the west side is a floor level tomb recess of similar date and style

14th century Sedilia in range with Piscina

Cusped cinquefoiled ogee heads with crockets and finials Detached cylindrical shafts, with moulded capitals and bases, separating three stepped seats and piscina

Banner cupboard

13th century sedilia

Statue niche (empty)

STONE
Fonts

Saxon drum or tub font
with lead-lined bowl decorated with crudely carved Latin crosses within arcading
Two bands of cable moulding above the stepped base

Norman pedestal font
with square bowl, in form of capital with roundels containing carved patterns alternating with large heads at corners
Short octagonal stem springing from drum pedestal on octagonal plinth
Remains of iron staple on rim for locking flat cover

Norman table font
with cup bowl, elaborately carved with chevron design around rim and with geometric motifs and stiff-leaf on body, supported on massive central cylindrical stem
Four angle shafts, rising from square plinth, outside the bowl, support projecting mask capitals against the sides of top of the bowl

Early English font
lead-lined hemispherical bowl, annulated with a band of continuous tendrils of foliage, carved in high relief, placed just below the rim
Plain cylindrical stem descends to a spreading foot, embellished with stylised acanthus leaves in high relief
Mounted on a millstone plinth

18th century font

Lead-lined bowl with a band of carved decoration around the rim; made up of four cherubs' heads with swags of drapery between

Below the rim the bowl tapers in a concave curve to a gadrooned calyx in high relief

Octagonal baluster stem with a band of carved anthemion leaves around the base

Stepped and moulded octagonal pedestal set on a shallow plinth

Late 19th century font (1873),
copied from 15th century font

Octagonal bowl with carved representations of the four Evangelists and their attributes, alternating with kneeling angels, each under a crocketed ogee canopy in the panels

Bosses of demi-angels at points of intersection beneath pinnacled buttresses which separate the panels

Octagonal stem ornamented with shields bearing symbols of the Passion on panels between engaged shafts

Oakleaf motifs in covered section beneath bowl

The moulded bases of the shafts stand on a stepped octagonal plinth standing on large stepped and moulded cruciform plinth of Mansfield stone

TEXTILES
Terms

All sorts of textiles are encountered in churches, some connected with church ritual, others with decoration or even the comfort of the congregation. Vestments are dealt with under *COSTUME* but all other ecclesiastical textiles, including **cloths, veils** and **kneelers** are considered here.

Since textiles in churches often involve work of devotion, specialist techniques, particularly embroidery and tapestry, are common on small scale objects like **kneelers** and on large scale objects like **wall hangings**, popular in modern churches. Fine quality materials were used for textiles in churches from the earliest times.

FABRICS

Brocade	generally silk, but may be gold, cotton or synthetic Woven with a raised pattern of coloured threads. Used for vestments, frontals and curtains
Cloth of gold	fabric with gold thread woven into the cloth
Cloth of silver	fabric with silver thread woven into the cloth
Cotton	any fabric from fine muslin to heavy canvas woven from the fibres of the cotton plant. Today generally used for altar linen and surplices
Damask	reversible, usually monochrome, with a self-pattern either abstract or of monograms, dates, arms etc. **Linen damask** used for towels; cotton and wool for curtains, pew seats etc silk for vestments and frontals
Garniture	fringes, tassels, knots, cords, etc
Kid	commonly used in 20th century appliqué work, gilded or silvered
Lace	fine open fabric made by hand or machine
Linen	woven from the fibres of flax. Cool to touch and slightly shiny. Originally always used for altar linen
Lurex	a metal-coloured thread/fabric much used today instead of genuine gold thread in church embroidery
Silk	woven from the thread produced by the larvae of the bombyxmori or bombycid moth. Woven into many rich fabrics used for vestments, frontals etc
Suede	undressed pigskin or kid, common in 20th century appliqué work
Synthetics	man made fabrics, woven from thread produced in a laboratory. Will not crease, so the thread often added to natural fibres as well as used on its own
Velvet	silk or cotton thread woven into a pile

DECORATIVE TECHNIQUES

Applied work or appliqué   the attaching of different fabrics, colours and shapes to a fabric

Crewel work   decorative embroidery with coloured wools on plain linen or twill ground

Canvas work   any type of stitch worked into holed canvas (eg for kneelers) This is **not** tapestry

Crochet   found in churches in the form of crochet lace, used as edging for communion cloths, super frontals and, sometimes, vestments

Gold work   the richest form of embroidery, using thread of fine gold paper wound round a core of silk. Other gold threads made from gold wire are

    Purl   like a coiled spring

    Bullion   large purl

    Passing   fine gold wire

    Pearl purl   tiny gold beads

    Plate   flat strips

    Spangles   thin pieces of shiny metal with a small hole for attachment

Patchwork   similar to inlaid but with symmetrical pieces

Quilting   two or more layers of material held together by stitched pattern, sometimes with cord inserted

Tapestry   fabric with a pictorial design, woven by a different technique from that of woven cloth. Can be hand or machine made. Usually found as wall hangings. The term should never be applied to canvas work embroidery

Whitework   generic term for embroidery worked in white thread on a white ground

TEXTILES
Embroidery Stitches

Couching	the tying down of one thread by another. Very many varieties. Generally used to edge a piece of applied work such as figure on a banner
Cross stitch	a cross either diagonal or vertical over 2 or 4 threads of canvas
Gros point or half cross stitch	goes over two threads diagonally
Petit point or tent stitch	goes over one thread diagonally
Hem stitch	used to fasten the hems of altar linen. It may be worked by hand or, with bought altar linen, by machine
Long and short stitch	forms a smooth surface. Used where shading is required
Satin stitch	commonly found forming the monograms on altar linen
Split stitch	seldom found on 20th century work but in earlier work used for hands and faces

Back

Blanket

Buttonhole

Chain

Chevron

Couching

Feather

Herringbone

Satin

Split

Cutwork

Darned netting

Drawn thread

Pattern darning

Quilting

Cross

Eye

Florentine

Gobelin

Hungarian

Italian

Mosaic

Parisian

Plait

Rice

Smyrna

Tent or petit point

Upright cross

Embroidered cope

of red silk damask decorated with applied crimson velvet, gold braid, green silk and canvas embroidered with gold thread, gold cord and silk in shades of green, yellow and brown: laid and couched work and metal spangles. The ground is powdered with fleurs-de-lys, sunbursts, stylised pineapples, scrolled foliage and the capital letter P surmounted by a crown.

On the false orphreys are ovals containing, at centre back, a Tudor rose and, down the sides, the initials SP (St Paul) alternating with the Sacred Monogram (IHS).

The round hood is trimmed with a fringe of gold thread and red silk and is attached to the cope by five silk and gold thread buttons. In the centre is an applied roundel with the Sacred Monogram IHS in Latin form, within a circle of rays; the same device appears on the **morse** (see page 44).

Most church lace is machine lace of the late 19th and early 20th centuries or 19th century hand-made lace applied to machine-made net. Earlier laces, however, were given to churches at the end of the 19th century and it is worth looking out for 17th century needle laces and 18th century bobbin laces. Machine-made lace was first introduced in the late 18th century.

Needlepoint lace
Developed from drawn-thread work, needlepoint lace is made with a single thread and needle, using embroidery stitches, dominated by buttonhole stitch.

Ecclesiastical robes and textiles are often adorned with **rose-point**, one of the many types of needlepoint, which consists of patterns worked in relief like sculptured work, forming strong and solid flowers and scrolls held in position by **brides** enriched with **picots.**

Pillow lace
Developed from knotted fringes and network, pillow lace is made with a multitude of threads wound upon bobbins stuck by pins into a pillow. The lace is created in a range of twists and plaits combining a varying number of threads, usually in or applied to a meshed ground. Where there is no **ground (fond or reseau)** the pattern is connected by **brides**.

Brides	bars or ties
Footing	straight edge or flouncing attached to material
Heading	scalloped or dentate free edge
Picots	small loops of twisted thread
Tallies	square or rectangular linking, characteristic of Buckinghamshire lace
Wheat ears	round or oval linking

TEXTILES
Veils and Cloths

CLOTHS

Dossal
(hanging back panel)
Riddel
(curtain hung on riddel-posts at back and sides of altar)
Super frontal
(embroidered and fringed)
Frontal
panelled (**orphreys**) and fringed
Fair linen cloth
with lace edging and embroidered
crosses

Laudian
(three or four sided throw-over altar frontal with motif on one side only)

Funeral pall
(usually black, purple or white, with motif in centre or on all sides, sometimes corners are slit)

VEILS

Chalice veil
(silk square veil used to cover communion chalice when not in use, changing in colour according to the season)

Ciborium or pyx veil
(white linen circular veil with hole in centre under which Sacrament is reserved)

Monstrance veil
(made of white silk, without lining, with plain hemmed edges, nearly twice the height of monstrance)

Humeral or offertory veil
(270 x 60cm)
(worn by priest when in procession or when moving the Sacrament; usually cream or white silk and lined)

Silk tabernacle veils
(in liturgical colours; divided in centre with hole for finial to protrude)

Aumbry veil   *covers door of aumbry; sometimes embroidered*
Lenten veil   *covers statues during Lent*

TEXTILES
Veils and Cloths

Bookmarker

Maniple
(approx 45cm long)

Burse
bellows style

Stole
(approx 120cm)

Burse
book style

(Maniples and stoles are double ended and have a central cross)

Alms bag

Pulpit or lectern fall
with motif in padded gold kid, gold threads and cords and artificial pearls

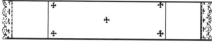

Fair linen cloth
(length and width of altar, usually with lace or embroidered designs on edges)

Communion linens

A   Corporal (50cm sq)
B   Communion veil, folded (45cm sq)
C   Palla (pl pallae) also called pall board (15 cm sq)
D   Purificator (30cm sq)
E   Lavabo towel (Anglican 60 x 27cm) (Roman Catholic 50 x 40cm)

Communion cloth
(small white linen napkin to catch crumbs)

Houselling cloth
(white linen, the length of the houselling bench (see page 175))

Kneelers or **hassocks** protect worshippers from discomfort while kneeling. **Cushions** will be found on the altar, on the pulpit desk and the sanctuary chair. Long **padded runners** will be used at the communion rail for kneeling worshippers or on benches for the seated congregation.

Pair of pale blue velvet wedding kneelers
on each a white silk satin-stitch embroidered dove

Kneeler with crossed keys embroidered in gold silk petit-point against a shaded grey wool gros-point field. Side edges covered completely with red wool cross stitch

Emerald green velveteen bench runner
with a bold fish design and water effect. Applied and embroidered in gold and silver kid leathers, cords and metallic threads

Red velvet altar cushion with corded edges and long tassels attached at the corners

TEXTILES
Flags and Banners

Knight's Banner

square (90cm sq) bearing the owner's arms over the whole surface. Banners may also be rectangular. In size they will conform to protocol: Princes' or Dukes' banners should be 123 cm sq; the Sovereign's banner should be 150 cm sq. The banner commonly known as the **Royal Standard** is correctly **The Sovereign's Banner**

Banner roll small square

Standard

either a long tapering flag split at the end, bearing the owner's device and motto (not arms or achievement) or an emblem on a staff

Pennant or pennon

small pointed flag with two or more streamers, born at the lance head
Gonfalon is similar but fixed to a bar
Vexillum scarf attached to a staff

Union Jack or Union Flag national ensign of the United Kingdom, combining the national banners of England, Scotland and Ireland, which may be flown on land by any British subject

Processional banner of the Mother's Union straight hung through loops. Figures of the Virgin and Child, in a combination of hand-worked appliqué and embroidery, against a pale blue ground. The name of the church at the top and the initials MU flanking the figures at the bottom. Blue and gold tasselled fringe

Colour	infantry regimental flag
Colours	pair of infantry regimental flags
Other banners	might show St George; arms of the see or parish; the arms of a guild or society connected with the parish

Carpets will be found on floors or as coverings for tables and benches. A carpet over 100 years old is antique, over 50 years old is semi-antique and anything from 25 years ago can be regarded as old. The most famous carpets come from Persia and Afghanistan but, since the 15th century, Persian carpets have been copied by Spain, Poland (notable for European coats of arms), France (particularly tapestry carpets) and England, where they were copied in tent and cross stitch in the 16th and 17th centuries. A fine carpet is judged by the quality of the wool; the tightness of the weave (in general the more knots per square inch, the better the quality); and the clarity and beauty of the design. The first step is to distinguish between pile, flat woven and embroidered carpets, then to recognise the main oriental carpet producing areas, before attempting to identify the individual types within the areas, which will be of town, village, or tribal origin.

CARPET TYPES

Afghanistan	wine-red field with large stylised patterns
Caucasian	large geometric designs enclosed in multicoloured diagonal bands; dragons; soft rose colour relieved by dark blue or black; ghiordes knot
Chinese	predominance of yellow; dragon, phoenix, lion, bat, cloud, swastika, pomegranate motifs
Indian	cotton; light pastel colours; French, Persian or Chinese style designs
Persian	repetitive all-over designs; central medallion, sometimes lobed or hung with festoons; decorated with pendants, lanterns and rectangular inscriptions; central motif often repeated at corners; gardens, hunting scenes and narratives (inc Biblical) popular; sehna and ghiordes knots
Turkish	small size; brilliant colours; borders with seven ribbons decorated with flowers; geometric patterns; representations of Islamic mosque arch; no picture narratives; little green
Turkoman	deep glowing red; geometric patterns with wavy brown outlines; repetitive octagons and hexagons divided in various ways, sometimes cross-wise into four parts arranged in parallel and perpendicular rows, known as **guls** (octagons) or **elephant's foot**

PERSIAN SUB-TYPES

Feraghan	rusty background; palmettes and vegetation; Herati pattern; thin; green borders
Hamadan	natural camelhair background; dark geometric medallions; tortoise motif; heavy; single knots
Herat	dark blue or purple red background; closed rosettes in elongated leaves, ribbon- pattern, scroll or diamond; rosette with eight points; green borders; very rich wool; rectangular shape; ghiordes or sehna knot
Heriz	light background; well spaced geometric patterns
Isfahan	bright background; symmetrical design; finely woven; round medallion with eight or sixteen points
Kashan	small flowers filling centre and borders; soft silky wool; bouquets resembling peacock feathers
Shiraz	tribal rugs; large medallion; stylised flowers, birds and animals
Tabriz	plain background; large central medallion, repeated and quartered at corners; four seasons pattern; hunting scenes; ghiordes or sehna knot

TEXTILES
Rugs and Carpets

KNOTS

Sehna knot
(pile thread twisted round one warp)

Ghiordes knot
(pile thread twisted around two warps)

Kelim
(threads incorporated into weaving so that rug can be used on either side)

Soumac weave

MAIN DESIGNS

Mihrab
(arch)

Medallion
(classical town design)

Overall
(tribal design)

Geometric
(village design)

BORDERS

Running dog

Crenellated

Tortoise

Recumbent S

T border

Wineglass

Writing

(in the borders) will be arabic, farsi, kufic, (or just decorative), telling the date, the maker, or quoting a text from the Koran

CARPET MOTIFS

Falcon Hour glass Hand Yin-Yang cycle

Bar medallion Anchor medallion

Vase Arabesques Palmette (Lotus)

Lily and iris Weeping willow Tulip Pomegranate

Elephant foot Octagon around barbed polygon Peony Cypress

TEXTILES
Rugs and Carpets

Dog

Tchi or cloud ribbon

Camel

Herati or Feraghan
pattern

Scorpion

Tortoise

Mir also called
Pear or Cone

Mir-i-boteh

Tree of life

Bokhara
candlesticks

Fish or acanthus
leaf

Water jug

Star of Solomon

Comb

Dragon and phoenix

One of the most common materials employed in churches, wood is chiefly used for furniture, either fixed or free standing. Until about 1660 most furniture was made from oak. In the 17th century walnut and exotic fruitwood inlays became popular along with beech, pine and cane. The end of the 17th century saw the development of gesso and lacquering techniques, upholstery and yew became more common. In the mid 18th century, the apogee of English furniture making, mahogany and then satinwood, finally replaced oak in fine furniture.

WOODS

Ash	light brown with yellowish streaky grain
Beech	very pale brown, with satiny grain prone to woodworm, sometimes stained to resemble walnut and other timbers Used for heavy country furniture
Chestnut	almost indistinguishable from oak
Elm	brown and tough, often used for Windsor chair seats
Mahogany	dark reddish brown, with slight grain. Not used before 1730
Oak	heavy hardwood which darkens with age, distinctive figures from medullary rays
Pine	yellow to red softwood. In use from 1660 and common in churches
Teak	light or dark brown, heavy and durable. In use in 20th century
Walnut	honey coloured (aged English wood) or darker red-brown (French and Italian) with tendency to woodworm. In use since 17th century
Yew	reddish to golden brown, very hard. Popular for country furniture

WOOD

CONSTRUCTION TECHNIQUES

Medieval furniture was held together by pegged mortise and tenon joints. Mouldings were cut in the solid and the corners turned with mason's mitres. From the mid 16th century, applied mouldings and mitred corners began to appear although pegged mortise and tenon joints were still used. From the mid 17th century joints ceased to be pegged. The dovetail joint, for carcase construction, was introduced c1660. Mouldings in 18th century furniture were generally applied and mitred.

Arris	sharp corner where two planes meet
Dovetailed	fan-shaped projections interlaced to form tight flat joint
Dowelled	round pins fitted into corresponding holes to make tight joint
Framed construction	based on use of mortise and tenon joint
Mitre	diagonal joint formed by two mouldings
Mortise	slot to receive projection **(tenon)** on another piece of wood
Tenon	projection protruded into mortise in another piece of wood
Boarded construction	planks held in place by nails, or pegged with oak pins at the angles and strengthened with crosspieces

WOOD
Terms

DECORATIVE TECHNIQUES

Applied Carving one piece of wood cut and applied to the surface of another wood cut or gouged out to leave shapes, which may be freestanding, in relief or pierced as tracery

Chip carving simple type of carved ornament used on wooden surfaces in the 13th, 14th and 15th centuries. The patterns, usually geometrical, were first set out with compasses and then chipped out, probably by the carpenter or joiner who made the chest. Chip carving persisted through the 16th and early 17th centuries

Cock beading small astragal or bead moulding applied to edges of drawer fronts

Cross banding strips of **veneer** at right angles to the rest of the surface

Dado rail wooden rail at height of chair backs on lower half of wall

Feather banding strips of **veneer** set diagonally to the rest of the surface

Incising cut or scratched into surface

Inlay design cut from thin veneers of other woods and fitted into prepared cavities in the surface

Marquetry complicated inlay designs, first fashionable in Holland and France

Mouldings strips of wood of various shapes with names of architectural origin

Parquetry geometric patterns inlaid or glued together to form a composite veneer

Pedestal supporting base for statue, object etc rising to height of dado

Skirting horizontal base board around bottom of wall

Stringing inlay of thin lines of wood or bone

Veneer thin sheet of richly **figured** (grained) wood, ivory or tortoiseshell glued to the surface of another material (see also **cross banding** and **feather banding**).

Surbase —

Pedestal — Plinth or base

Baldacchino
(canopy over altar, throne or doorway)

Bracket
(decorative or functional support for object)

Console
(any bracket or corbel of scrolled form)

Console
(desk-like frame of organ, containing keyboards, stops etc)

Bracket
pierced and pinnacled in the form of a flying buttress

Console mirror
(mirror supported by bracket against wall)

Oxford frame
(type of frame for pictures and texts, with the horizontal and vertical members forming a cross at each corner. Crossed ends of this type were used on hymn boards in churches in the 1830s)

Console table
(table supported by bracket against wall)

WOOD

WOOD

Claw and ball   Hoof   Paw or hair claw   Pad

Ball   Bun   Turnip   Club

Spade   Marlborough   Stump   Stump

Knurl, spanish or caterpillar   Scroll   Gutta   Peg

18th century bracket   Splayed bracket   Ogee bracket   Cabriole bracket

16th century
Cup and cover

17th century
Cup and cover

Columnar
c1620

Fluted c1630

Bobbin turned
c1660

Square moulded
c1665

Ball turned
c1670

Columnar c1670

Ball and
bead c1670

Barley sugar twist or
spiral-turned c1670

Double scroll or
inverted c1685

Umbrella c1690

Turned
tapered c1690

Square chamfered
(inside) from 1740

18th century
Cabriole

18th century
Broken cabriole

WOOD
Legs

Cluster column or grouped pillar c1760

Carved or applied fret c1765

Square tapered c1775

18th century Hipped cabriole

Fluted vase stem Late 17th century

Pierced fret c1790

Reeded columnar c1803

Sabre c1815

Vase-shaped, slab standard or trestle

Cruciform

Tripod foot on stem

Splayed, split and wedged through seat

Arched stretcher

Box stretchers

Cowhorn, spur, crinoline or hooped stretcher

Flat and serpentine cross stretcher

Shaped and joined by turned crossbar

Flat incurved stretcher

Floor level stretchers

H-stretcher

Rounded H-stretcher centred on baluster

Double H-stretcher with sausage turnings

18th century H-stretcher

X-stretcher

Scrolled X-stretcher centred on a coronet

Scrolled X-stretcher

Curved vertical X-stretcher

Curved horizontal X-stretcher

Wavy

WOOD

WOOD
Panels

Most panels are bevelled or rebated to fit into a groove in the surrounding framework. Mouldings may be added (**bead** moulding or **bolection** moulding) to conceal the junction of the panel with the framework. **Wainscoating** is the term generally used for wood panelling on walls up to **dado** height.

Coffered panels have a deeply sunk surface below the level of the framework, differing from **sunk panels** which are shallower.

Styles of panelling have been copied in different periods.

15th century
Gothic *(pierced)*

15th and 16th centuries
Gothic *(pierced)*

Early 16th century
Parchment

Early 16th century
Linenfold

Romayne
c1530-1550

Mid 16th century
Renaissance

From 18th century
Fielded *(raised)*

From 18th century
Coffered

19th and 20th centuries
Applied Gothic tracery

ALTAR AND COMMUNION RAILS

19th or 20th century purpose built Altar

Rectangular frame with plain overhanging Altar-top incised with five Consecration crosses, set on a projecting cornice. Front divided into three bays, back open, sides and each bay of the front contain, at the top, pierced tracery panels with two cusps below the arch and spandrel panels following the shape of the top of the bays Most of the members of the framework, which stands on a base of rails are chamfered on the outside

Remember to record the line of the joints. Similar constructions, usually hidden by the frontal, often have the fronts and sides panelled with applied Gothic tracery, the back being left open

Communion rail

Sloped capping with moulded edges raised on solid end-supports shaped and cut with ogee sections along one side: the supports are braced by a medial top rail and rest on base runners of ogee design bearing a kneeling board which has been set on oak blocks to allow a restful posture, the joints are pegged

Houselling benches

Long wooden benches with a flat table/stool top. Used as communion rails, sometimes with a kneeler along one of the long sides. Can be used with a **Houselling cloth** draped across the top. Height approx 60cm

WOOD
Furniture

BENCHES, PEWS AND CONFESSIONALS

Benches are seats with supports whereas pews are enclosed or elevated seating. The backs of benches usually have open rails or panels and will often have **bookrests** fitted to them for the use of the occupants of the bench behind. Post-Reformation bookrests are usually sloping. Each section of benches will probably include a bench front or desk. Bench ends are often decorated with carvings and finials usually called **poppyheads**.

Pews have panels, doors and benches and may be raised above the floor or canopied or furnished and heated. Some are painted or carved with the names or coats of arms of families. The most popular material was oak until the 19th century when pine examples also appeared.

Stalls are individual or multiple seats placed against or sometimes **returned** *(at right angles)* against a wall or screen. Some have tabernacled canopies, or traceried backs and cornices and nearly all have shaped side-panelling sometimes with carved or applied elbows. The stall fronts (or **desks**) may be traceried and have poppyheads. Tip-up seats known as **misericords**, may be ornately carved on the underside. Subsidiary carvings on either side of the main projection are known as **supporters**.

Bench with close boarded back, moulded top rail and curved ends to the seat
Carved rectangular bench-end
Unicorn below an arch supporting a pomegranate with branches flowing from top of stem to top of arch
Plain gouged blind arcade below

Bench front with integral kneeler and level bookrest
Rectangular arch-topped end with lively 16th century carving incorporating two quatrefoils below a Pelican in her Piety and a foliated poppyhead
Colonnade of trefoil headed arches between top and bottom rails, with pierced triangular spandrels

Open backed bench with two rails and one shaped end with simple, moulded edging the other end flush with wall

Stalls of four bays with a canopy formed of a cusped ogee arch over each stall, decorated with flame-like crockets and fleur-de-lys finials and supported by moulded shafts from the shoulder rail
Moulded scrolled elbows
Misericords carved on the underside with a Green Man

17th century Squire's or family pew

18th century box pews

CONFESSIONAL

Cresting

Finial

Cornice

Frieze

Console

Lintel

Architrave

Reeded pilasters

Recessed panels

Plinth

Confessional

(possibly adapted from an Elizabethan internal porch) of square frame and panel construction of armoire style, with reeded pilasters on pedestals with recessed panels. The rails of the door carved with a geometric lined motif, the muntins and stiles with guilloche, the architrave with irregular chevrons, the fielded panels plain except for the horizontal top panel which bears a foliated scroll carving tied at the centre. There is large palmette carving on the lintel and the console brackets supporting the entablature are carved with leaves, the frieze is enriched with mitred lozenge moulding surmounted by dentil moulding, the latter omitted on the sides of the pew.

The sides do not have any enrichment below the frieze and consoles; on one side is a metal grille set in a panel at eye-level for someone kneeling.

Above the moulded cornice are dog-like corner finials, squatting on square plinths and holding shields between their paws; crestings of coats-of-arms amidst floriated scrolls and fleur-de-lys are set between them.

BOXES

Feretory
(container for saint's relics)
Metal rod across the gabled top
secures the hasp and has eyelets
for attaching priest's neck cord
Pierced round and rectangular
apertures in roof and sides

16th century oak alms box
Rectangular with domed lid bound
with iron straps and decorated
with enamelled tracery

17th century oak alms box
Rectangular with carved
date and inscription on
front:
1684/
REMEMBER/
THE PORE
in contemporary lettering,
and supported by a
bracket decorated with
leaves. Also found in the
18th century

17th century poor box
Oak post, the top hollowed to
form a box
Lid with coin slot has three iron
straps hinged at front and
secured to post by padlocks
Simple applied moulding runs
around three sides of the post

WOOD

17th century desk-type oak Bible box
Flat top, sloping flap with butterfly hinges.
Typical Lake District style interlace carving
on the front flanking a keyplate above the
date 1675
Neatly moulded edges
Document drawers *(upright)* within

17th century rectangular Bible box
with original lock and hasp
Two large lunettes carved on front
enclosing stylised leaf decoration and
similar motifs in spandrels

20th century Book of Remembrance stand
Desk top with glazed viewing panel,
supported on a metal frame of a pair of
standards united by two stretchers and
fixed to the rear base of the desk
The feet curving forward to take balance

20th century Book of Remembrance stand in Gothic style
Table style box with glazed top above
carved frieze of running vine leaf ornament
Rectangular panels of reticulated tracery
running between legs on all four sides
immediately below frieze and with blank
shield at centre front
Shelf unites the four legs of square section

CHESTS

Medieval dugout chest
Hollowed log with solid slab lid, strengthened by five iron bands and strap hinges, provision for three locks and two padlock loops which were probably later additions

13th century cope chest
Quadrant shaped with frame of stout posts at corners into which rails are tenoned
Lid in two halves with ornate scrolled and foliated iron hinges and decoration
Panels of sides nailed into rebates in frame

Early 14th century chest
Front and back tenoned into wide stiles extended to provide legs
Iron straps, binding the chest with bifurcated decorative ends
Chains with rings suspended from them, fixed to the sides

Flanders chest 1550-1600
Front of two wide vertical stiles and two wide horizontal planks
Traces of painted decoration in fantastic bestiary scenes on the stiles
Between the stiles the front is decorated with curvilinear blind tracery

WOOD
Furniture

14th-16th century chest

Massive planks pegged into corner posts of square section raising chest from floor strengthened by angled iron straps and flat straps (which strengthen the breaks in the timber)

Strap hinges continuing across top hinged to hasps and locks

16th century counter

Chest with long legs about table height

Top sometimes scored

Early 17th century hutch chest

Frame and panel construction with five panels at front and two at the sides decorated with simple linenfold. Two of the front panels were originally doors but are now secured to the frame

Top of chest sawn and hinged for access

Two stretchers run across the length of the chest at floor level

— Cornice
— Frieze
— Pilaster strips

Late 17th century dole cupboard
Stamped enrichment on cornice
Geometric inlay on frieze
Two doors, each with six turned spindles in two stages
Pilaster strips carved with stiff leaves

17th century mule chest
(shallow type of panelled chest with drawers in lower part)

18th century mortsafe
(earlier mortsafes usually lidless and of stone)

Late 18th century mahogany chest of drawers
Serpentine-fronted chest with oversailing top and cross-banded canted corners, three long drawers with cockbeading, swan-necked Rococo brass handles and C-scrolled escutcheons
A slide above the top drawer
Splayed feet with bow-shaped apron on front and sides

WOOD
Furniture

Mid 19th century walnut Davenport

Scrolled front uprights supporting scrolled flap, four drawers on left side and cupboard door concealing three drawers on other side
Ink drawer on left
Bun feet
Use of term 'Davenport' sufficient to describe the style

19th century military chest

With brass corners and sunken handles, usually mahogany (upper stage sometimes a **secretaire**)

19th and 20th century frontal chest

Hinged top-opening to enable frontals to be hung on rods
105cm x 300cm x 30cm
Usually of softwood

19th and 20th century linen and vestment press

Usually of softwood

CHAIRS

Chair of state c1600
Armchair of horizontal X-frame construction, closely covered in crimson velvet, trimmed with fringed gold gallon and garnished with gilt-headed nails and fitted with down stuffed cushion covered en suite

Pediment or cresting
Tongue
Outer volute
Spandrel
Earpiece
Roundheaded arch in panelled back
Backpost
Scrolled arm
Upholstered seat
Combined front leg and arm support
Seat rail
Stretcher

Mid 17th century chair
Panel back construction, panel carved with roundheaded arch decorated with scrolled foliage
Scrolled pediment with tongues protruding beside outer volutes carved with foliage and central roundel
Carving similar to that on the back, on earpieces and back-posts above scrolled arms
Turned front uprights of baluster form sectioned by blocked joints
Seat upholstered in red figured velvet with various reinforcements (later modifications)
Plain renewed stretchers
In chairs of this type, the backs are sometimes raked, seats splayed, stretchers and front uprights vary in form

WOOD
Furniture

Glastonbury chair c1630
Chair with panel back and X-shaped legs joined by crossbar. Shaped arms from seat to back, both held by wooden pins
The only description required, beyond 'Glastonbury', is the rake of the back, shape of the arms and decoration, which may be on both the inside and rear of the back and arms, the wood, measurements and date

— Finials
— Upper rail of back
— Arcaded back
— Applied split balusters on back uprights
— Baluster columns
— Lower rail of back
— Front stretcher

Oak armchair of box form mid 16th century
Square back, surmounted at either end by the figure of a crouching lion, with an oblong panel of finely carved Renaissance design consisting of male and female terminal figures supporting a trophy of arms, their tails ending in scrolls
Below are two rectangular linenfold panels
Flat arms enclose plain panels
Lower part of the back is fitted behind with a cupboard door
Two linenfold panels in front of the box of simpler design than those on the back

Mid 17th century chair
Arcaded back, the upper rail having three arches with carved and incised decoration and cusping supported by two baluster columns resting on a lower rail with leafy scrolls; the upper rail surmounted by two, and the lower by three knob finials. The back uprights have crozier-shaped finials and applied split baluster ornaments. Spirally turned front stretcher, the rest plain. Front legs have new feet: back legs slotted for castors. Seat sunk for a squab cushion
Arcaded back common in Yorkshire and Derbyshire

WOOD

Late 17th or 18th century settle

Top rail of back treated with lunettes

Lozenge carving in four-panelled back

Lozenge decoration used from about 1620s especially common second half of 17th century

Backstool 1680-1720

Flat pyramidal caps to backposts

Lunette cresting carved with a tulip amidst sprawling foliage above similar carving with a dog-rose on rectangular panel

Opening below panel

Moulded seat rails

Turned front legs

Bobbin-turned front rail stretcher

Walnut armchair c1670

The cresting of the back and of the rail joining the front cabriole legs is elaborately carved in openwork with putti crowning a female figure, flanked by putti blowing trumpets

Spiral uprights with crowned female head finials

Lion couchant on each armrest

Sides of the back adorned with openwork carvings of putti amidst vines and roses growing from baskets

Original canework back; seat (formerly caned) upholstered in green velvet

WOOD
Furniture

Beech chair c1690

Tall back with moulded arched cresting rail, with ears, and straight back rail enclosing five vertical moulded spars
Front seat rail has veneered and shaped apron, hidden by fringe of red Victorian plush covering the slightly tapered seat
Turned front legs with ball feet, united by a turned front stretcher rail
Turned H-stretchers unite all four legs, the back legs being slightly splayed
Mouldings where back uprights join cresting rail, have been carefully mitred at each corner

Yoke or top rail

Back upright

Baluster or vase splat
Shoe

Knee
Apron rail

Early 18th century side chair

Splat back with serpentine top rail, cabriole front legs with pad feet, wavy apron rail and no underframing
Drop-in tapestry covered seat

Mid 19th century hall chair
Oval back supported on C scrolls of
X-frame construction
The rococo scrolls of the back and
the tied X are ornamented with carved
acanthus decoration
Seat has heavily fluted seat rails

19th and 20th century church chair
Beech frame and elm or rush seat
Top rail usually shaped *(yoked in
illustration)*
Middle rails often bowed
Elm seats are usually saddle shaped
Book pocket between backposts
Box stretchers with attached shelf
for kneeler

WOOD
Furniture

COUNTRY STYLE CHAIRS

Windsor chairs

The most popular country chair design of the 19th century is very distinctive and often found in churches. Windsor chairs come in many shapes but usually have elm seats, beech spindles (struts, stays or rods), beech legs and stretchers, and ash bowed parts. The legs and supports are pegged into the seat; the legs are splayed. In some examples, two stays form a brace from the top of the back to a bobtail projecting from the rear of the seat. A horizontal hoop forms a semi-circle across the back and along to the front as arm supports. Every variant of style has a name, for example, if the hoop is missing and the back bowed, the chair is a **Single-bowed Windsor**. Most Windsor chairs were made in Buckinghamshire.

Hoopback
Windsor

Gothic hoopback
Windsor

Lowback
Windsor

Tablet top
Windsor

Comb back
Windsor

**Bow back
Windsor**

Bow

Splat (wheelback)

Stays

Bobtail (hidden)

Front upright

Saddle seat

Spur stretcher

WOOD

18th century yew
Gothic Windsor armchair
Arch bow
Ash saddle seat
Cabriole legs
Club feet
Crinoline (spur) stretcher and
turned back supports

19th century
Mendlesham Windsor armchair
Low back with double crest rail of square
section infilled with three turned balls
Vase-shaped splat flanked by three sticks
Flat outward curving arms extending
beyond sloping supports
Saddle seat, splayed legs and H-stretcher

Smoker's Bow
Windsor c1860
Double H-stretcher

Lath back
Windsor

High back
Ladderback

WOOD
Furniture

CHAIRBACKS

Queen Anne

Prince of
Wales feather

Fiddle

Shield

Ladder

Square

Lyre

Riband

Gothic

Oval
late 18th century

Balloon
19th century

Gothic style
19th century

Shouldered balloon
19th century

Elizabethan style
19th century

Spoon hall seat
19th century

WOOD

WOOD
Furniture

DOORS

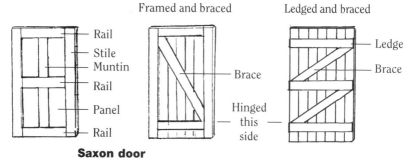

Framed and braced

Ledged and braced

Rail
Stile
Muntin
Rail
Panel
Rail

Brace

Hinged
this
side

Ledge

Brace

Saxon door
ledged vertical boards backed by horizontal
boards

ledge

ledge

Saxon doors were fastened together
by long wrought-iron nails with
ornamental heads, driven through
the door and clenched on the inside
Ledges were always confined to the
back or inside of the door

In the 12th century, although
construction techniques were
similar, doors were often decorated
by the smith with wrought-iron
hinges, locks, handles and knockers
The hinges usually have bifurcated
ends and stamped work of
contemporary design

**Norman
door**
with
alternating
horizontal
hinges with
double
scrolled
bifurcated
terminals

The smith declined in prominence in
the 14th century and decoration on
doors came into the realm of the
carpenter. Locks and hinges were
plainer. Besides mouldings or cover
beads to cover the joints, tracery was
either carved into the woodwork or
applied with glue and nails

In the late 17th century the smith's
craft enjoyed a slight revival and
decorated hinges reappeared. Many
churches have 19th century doors,
often exact copies of earlier doors
but the decoration on the later doors
tends to be thicker, more precise
and regular

**14th to late
17th century
door**

**14th century
door**
with applied
reticulated tracery

WOOD

FONT COVERS

In the medieval period, wooden font covers (often highly decorative) were fitted to fonts to protect the Holy water. Medieval font covers were copied in the 19th century as part of the Gothic Revival movement. Octagonal shapes, which had a mystical connotation, were frequently used in Gothic work.

Crown font cover 17th and early 18th century

Simple octagonal flat cover moulded at the edge, supporting eight ogee scrolls rising from the angles and meeting at the head of a central baluster-shaped post, just below the bulb final The volute of each scroll is carved with a rosette on both sides

Cone font cover

Lightly moulded octagonal base with moulded ribs, enclosing flat panels. Each rib decorated with three crockets and rising from each of the eight angles to the neck, surmounted by a four-tier finial

Font cover

Pinnacled and spired in three stages incorporating telescopic device for lifting by font crane

Highest stage lofty crocketed pinnacle with gables at base and finial top, supported on five slender annulated columns

Middle stage cruciform in plan, with four slender annulated compound columns at centre, flanked by eight slender annulated columns in pairs supporting a roof with four projecting crocketed gables

Lowest stage square in plan; at each angle flying diagonal buttresses culminating in crocketed pinnacles; at each side a panel carved with two foliage filled quatrefoils below, and above, an open pointed arch with bead moulding on the extrados and enclosing geometrical tracery, supported on slender central annulated columns; the crown of the arch breaking into a crocketed gable with a pierced trefoil in its upper angle. Inside, painted figures of Christ kneeling and John the Baptist standing

Base with a band of moulding formed from a geometrical pattern of mostly circular indentations, and with a band of imbricated decoration inclined inwards

WOOD
Furniture

PULPITS AND DESKS

Frieze
Sounding board or tester
Pendant finial

Stile
Desk
Cornice
Top rail
Hand rail
Capped finial
Newel post
Baluster
Winder
Tread
Riser

Panel
Stem
Plinth

15th century oak pulpit

Octagonal drum, the panels on each of the six visible facets richly carved with blind tracery, consisting of cinquefoil ogee arches, crocketed top edge, but no finials

The spandrels have trefoil tracery flanking the ogee arches

The two arches are subdivided by a centre stile

Desk made from 15th or 16th century oak with carved edges

19th century stem with attached brackets on octagonal plinth

19th century hexagonal sounding board with pendant finials at each angle and frieze of scrolled carving

19th century stairway of four threads on S side

Plain rectangular newel post with pyramidal capped finial, grooved hand rail and plain balusters

WOOD

18th century three decker pulpit

Sounding board

Pulpit

Lectern

Clerk's desk

19th century oak lectern *(see also METAL: Lecterns page 124)*
Desk supported on solid cruciform brackets with shaped and bevelled edges, each bracket pierced in the centre with a quatrefoil
Stem of clustered shafts with annulets attached to rectangular central shaft
Cruciform base with plain sill and similar brackets to those above

Desk

Apron

Kneeler

Runner
or side-rail

Panel with
inscription

Bottom front rail

Litany desk, prie-dieu or faldstool

Credence
(see page 11)

WOOD
Furniture

RAILS

Moulded oak top rail
Wrought-iron cylindrical supports
(or **standards**) with spiral-twist
centre sections between knots, and
ivy decorated brackets splaying
either side of upper one-third:
octagonal buttressed bases
Bottom oak sill forms integral
kneeler

Moulded top rail
with incised lunettes on frieze
Pillar-turned balusters between
sturdier standards of the same shape
which have cup and cover finials
Grooved and domed bottom rail
tenoned into bases of standards,
the balusters resting on the rail

17th century Laudian
(enclosing altar) **communion rail**

Gallery (or tribune)
with balustrade consisting of groups
of five turned balusters separated by
fluted stiles. Festooned frieze below
moulded sill.
*West galleries common from late
16th century until 19th century
Later ones have panelled fronts*

SCREENS

Screens, particularly those which divided the chancel from the centre of the church, were an essential part of medieval religious practice. The congregational principles of the Reformation led to the wholesale destruction of chancel screens which were not generally reintroduced until the 19th century. Screens or **parcloses** were also used, to separate side chapels and other areas of the church.

On rood screens, the Rood figures are usually placed centrally with the cross on a tall pedestal and the flanking figures on small pedestals. Original groups are very rare, though a few survive in Wales, and most date from the religious revival of the 1840s. Many were polychromed and a torch or magnifying glass often reveals traces of original colour in the corners and recesses. Where the chancel arch was boarded in above the rood screen, the resultant tympanum was sometimes painted with a Doom scene showing the division of souls into Heaven or Hell.

Screens are usually divided into a series of bays with an opening which may or may not be gated. The outer bays are generally panelled at the base and open, except for the posts, between the **transom** *(centre)* **rail** and the **head** *(top)* **rail**. The heads of the **lights** *(openings)* usually have pierced carved tracery.

Bressumer beam	horizontal beam supporting main superstructure
Ceilure	section of roof directly above a rood screen, (or an altar), sometimes richly decorated as canopy to the rood
Chancel screen	dividing chancel from nave
Chantry screen	dividing tomb from chancel or nave
Parclose screen	separating chapel from body of church
Quire screen or pulpitum	dividing eastern section of cruciform church from body of church (opposite rood screen)
Rood	cross or crucifix
Rood beam	beam spanning chancel arch supporting **rood** *(Christ on the Cross)*
Rood screen	screen incorporating Christ on the Cross invariably flanked by figures of Mary and St John
Roodloft	space above vaulted or coved rood screen which supports gallery fronts at east and west sides
Tower screen	separating tower from nave

WOOD

WOOD
Furniture

Billets
Cornice

Top rail

Pierced head-
ings to lights

Cap
Post

Bay of two
lights

Transom rail

Panel with
blind tracery

Muntin

Plinth

Screen

of four bays, the opening in second bay from north end
Heavy overhanging cornice crested with billet moulding, below which are
moulded fillets enclosing two bands of frieze, the upper one carved with
pellets and gadrooning, the lower with an undulating vine; below are more
bands of stepped moulding resting on the top rail
Each bay contains two lights, between slender reeded posts with cinqefoil
heads and pierced tracery beneath pointed arches with trefoil piercing in
the spandrels of the upper arches
The lower stage, either side of the passageway, has blind cinquefoil headed
arches applied to the fielded panels
All frame members have applied mouldings

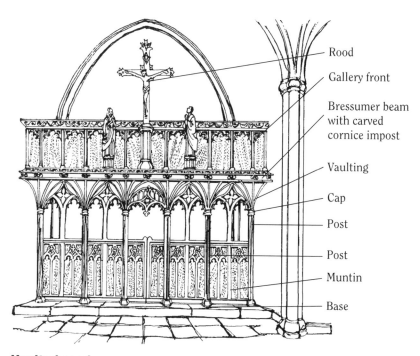

Rood

Gallery front

Bressumer beam
with carved
cornice impost

Vaulting

Cap

Post

Post

Muntin

Base

WOOD

Vaulted rood screen

of five bays, the centre bay having a pair of doors, gallery front on the
west side

Central cross on tall octagonal pedestal with cap and base and carved
ornamental terminals to the arms and pierced tracery at the central
intersection. The label with INRI appears above the head of the
traditionally carved Christus, figures of the Blessed Virgin Mary and St
John flank the Crucifix, both have their hands clasped in prayer, their
heads and shoulders protruding above the panelling, stand on reeded
pedestals

The rood beam is carved with two rows of carved ornament (flowing
foliage over deep hollow paterae) spaced over each post and arch

Reeded posts carry the ribbed vaulting beneath the loft which is
panelled, with a blind cinquefoil headed arch in each of the ten full
and two half panels, surmounted by a cornice of carved running
ornament

Above the transom rail there are five bays, each with a two-light
cinquefoil headed opening united with a central quatrefoil beneath
a pointed arch. Beneath the transom rail the panels are carved with
blind trefoil headed arcading. The centre bay is wider than side
bays with a pair of doors to the height of the transom rail, each
with full panels decorated as side bays, but with posts which meet
and rise above the transom rail to form a finial on each door

WOOD
Furniture

STOOLS

Chairs developed from more simple stool shapes but never completely supplanted stools. Early inventories distinguish between highstools, lowstools, foot stools and elbow *(arm)* or back *(side)* chairs. The medieval backstool, in use until the late 18th century, is the hybrid with most in common with stools and chairs.

Backstool c1600

Oak form c1520
of plank construction
Apron, extending beyond solid supports to ends of seat, is of ogee shape with rounded ends
Supports have moulded edges and arched openings below

Joined stool from 1550
Four turned legs splayed outwards united by a rail beneath the seat linked by floor level stretchers
(19th century coffin stools are similar but with longer legs)

Early 17th century folding X-type faldstool

Baroque stool with Braganza feet c1690
Arched and scrolled central stretcher, two turned side stretchers with block central section

TABLES

14th-16th century oak trestle table
Plank top supported by trestles with ogee opening at base
Pair of central stretchers with protruding tenons secured by wooden wedges

Elizabethan oak drawleaf table c1600
Moulded frieze with deeply carved diagonal gadrooning
Four bulbous legs with cups carved with acanthus and gadrooned covers
Rectangular section floor-level stretchers
Gadrooning often referred to as nulling

Jacobean oak table c1640
Top formed of three planks with apron, six thin tapered turned legs joined by square section stretchers

17th century country oak side table
Inlaid banding of fruit wood let into solid oak around top and drawer
Wide apron rail of William and Mary style with cockbeading around the edge
Neatly turned legs of baluster shape
Joints pegged
Barley sugar twist H-stretchers

WOOD
Furniture

Oak side table c1670
Frame of halved hexagonal shape with circular top folded in centre
Gate at rear with square section stretcher six turned baluster legs
Halved hexagonal bottom board

Stuart dresser
c1680

Gate-leg table
c1730

D-end table
c1780

Pembroke table
c1800

Sofa table
c1820

20th century credence (see also page 11)
Moulded top-rail stretcher between plain pillar trestles with chamfered corners, to which is attached an ogee shaped apron carved with cursive lilies
Plain moulded domed bottom stretcher

Beadle's mace

Constable's truncheons

Collection plate

Collection ladles

OBJECTS

The clock in the tower (with or without an external dial) is known as a **turret** or **tower clock**. Most dioceses have a Clocks Adviser who may be contacted through the Secretary of the Diocesan Advisory Committee. Vestries may contain a variety of domestic clocks, which may be broadly divided into two classes, **wall hanging** and **free standing**.

Wall hanging
The commonest wall clock is the **dial clock**, spring driven and contained in a circular wooden case, occasionally with a downward extension to accommodate a longer pendulum. **Tavern** or **Act of Parliament clocks** have a long trunk section to accommodate weights and a long pendulum. **Lantern** or **hooded clocks** may occasionally be found.

Free standing
The most usual free standing clocks are **mantel** or **bracket clocks** which are spring driven and stand upon a mantelpiece, or other horizontal surface. **Long-case** or **grandfather clocks** are less likely to be found, these are weight driven and stand on the floor.

In addition, some clocks are built into galleries or other parts of the structure. The maker's name will usually give a clue to the date but only if features of the clock and case support his dates. Baillie's and Loomes's books are useful *(see FURTHER READING)*, but there are still omissions and as different generations of a family often had the same christian names, confusion can occur.

Bob	weight at end of pendulum
Dial	clock face
Fret	pierced brass decoration on lantern clocks or sound aperture on later clocks
Fusée	grooved cone to equalise power of mainspring
Hood	top section of longcase clock which generally lifts or slides off
Lenticle	glass let into the door of a longcase clock to allow motion of bob to be seen; less common by c1710
Movement	working parts of clock
Weights	cylindrical lead, cast iron or brass cased weights hung from chains or other lines

Hooded clock
with weights
c1745

Lantern clock
with weights
c1680

Tavern or Act of Parliament clock
late 18th century weight-driven and unglazed

CLOCKS

CLOCKS
Types

WALL HANGING CLOCKS
Dial clocks
Cases are ebonised or of common furniture woods, while some early 19th century ones have brass or mother of pearl inlay. Later examples of German or American clocks have fancy inlay bandings and usually have a downward extension with a glazed door showing the pendulum. Clocks with this extension are known as **drop dial clocks**.

Dials: Early ones may be of silvered brass and some painted wooden specimens survive. The vast majority are made of painted iron, some convex but most flat. German and American clocks have dials of painted zinc.

Movements: English movements have a fusée and only a few strike. German and American clocks have open springs, no fusées and usually strike.

FREE STANDING CLOCKS
Longcase clocks
Cases are made of the same woods and have the same designs and mouldings as furniture, but mahogany is rare before 1750. In general later ones are taller and broader than early examples, but many cottage clocks follow smaller, simpler, early designs.

Dials: 17th century dials are small and square, but later ones usually larger. **Break-arch dials** are normal from c1715, but many square dials continued to be made, especially for cottage clocks, which often had only one hand until almost the end of the 18th century. Painted dials were introduced c1775 but did not entirely supplant engraved brass.

Movements: Eight-day and longer duration movements almost invariably rely on catgut, metal or nylon lines to support weights. 30 hour clocks usually have a single weight on an endless chain or rope.

Dial clock
English c1850
Painted flat dial
non-striking
mahogany case

Gabled pediment
Hood
Fret
Square headed trunk door
Trunk
Lenticle showing pendulum bob
Base
Plinth

Late 17th century architectural longcase clock with square dial

Bracket or mantel clocks

In the 18th century, most examples will be English. In the 19th century French clocks are common while German and American copies of both occur in late 19th century.

Cases: English examples use the same woods as longcases, French ones often gilt metal or marble (sometimes slate). Some American clocks have cast iron cases.

Dials: English dials are smaller versions of longcase dials, normally without seconds; French dials are usually circular.

Movements: English, French and the best German examples are good quality, American ones less so.

TURRET CLOCKS: See further reading

Lunar dial

Spandrels

Case

Date aperture

Chapter ring, brass, often silvered, on which the numbers are engraved

Plinth

Bracket feet

18th century mahogany bracket or mantel clock

Arched ornamental dial showing phases of the moon, asymmetrical rococo spandrels, key escutcheon and matching blind escutcheon and corner pieces flanking the lunar dial
Wavy minute hand
Arabic minute figures, plain silvered chapter ring and large date aperture
Maker's name at base of applied chapter ring

CLOCKS

MONUMENTS
Terms

Monuments inside churches range from large, elaborate canopied monuments to modest tablets affixed to the wall. The latter may simply carry inscriptions or they may include sculpture, carving and elaborate decoration. Costumed figures, lettering, symbols, heraldry and architectural features all appear on monuments and memorials. Many early monuments were coloured. Sadly, it is rare for any original colour to have survived, but later restorers have sometimes attempted to return medieval monuments to the rich hues in which they first appeared.

Monuments are full of clues to the history of the church and its community. They can tell us about the people who lived around the church and what they looked like; how wealthy the community was and why; how and why people died in different periods and many other details of their lives. They are also full of information on contemporary artistic style, philosophy and religious observance.

In the medieval period, all monuments stood on the floor, either against the wall or away from it. Wall monuments, entirely supported on the wall, were virtually unknown before the 16th century. Floor monuments were either large structures or simple floor slabs and generally lay over the mortal remains of the person or family they commemorate. Wall monuments, on the other hand, mostly consist of a tablet bearing an inscription in an architectural frame or cartouche, usually placed close to where the body had been interred.

Over time, monuments tend to have been moved around the church and may be nowhere near their original site.

Achievement
Pediment — Nowy-headed tablet
Cornice
Shoulders
Tablet with inscription
Flanking pilasters — Rectangular tablet with arched head
Wings
Apron with blank shield
Brackets

Inscriptions

AMDG	[ad majorem Dei Gloriam]	to the greater Glory of God
HIS	[hic iacet sepultus]	here lies buried
HMP	[hoc monumentum posuit]	he erected this monument
INST	[in nomine Sanctae Trinitatis]	in the Name of the Holy Trinity
MS	[memoriae sacrum]	sacred to the memory

Floor Slabs pre 1300 — Slabs tapered from head to foot and were usually of local materials but Purbeck marble was commonly used for quality work. In the 12th century, slabs were ornamented with a variety of designs, carved in low relief or incised, often with a cross or symbol to indicate the profession of the deceased, but usually without lettering. Particularly after 1200, the slab might have borne a representation of the deceased in stone or later in brass but not a likeness *The same figure may be found in different churches*

13th-17th centuries — Brasses, made of thin plates of copper/zinc alloy, were commonly set flush into the stone. Often only the indent of the brass survives today, the original having been lost or destroyed, but even a worn indent should give an idea of at least the shape of the brass. *Indents from which the brass is missing should be carefully described as they are of great interest*

17th and 18th centuries — Massive slabs of marble or bluish-grey stone were widely used, often with an achievement in bas-relief and an incised inscription in roman lettering

19th century — The making of figured brasses for monuments was revived as part of a general movement towards medieval revival but slabs of a wide variety of materials and styles are found

| 12th century stone coffin lid with cross in relief | 13th century slab with incised fleurée cross and fish and key symbols | 14th century slab with indent of demi-figure, panel and two shields | 17th century grey marble with bas-relief achievement in roundel above inscription |

Tomb-chests

Tomb-chests are found with or without an effigy lying on top. They may be free-standing or recessed under a canopy against a wall
Free-standing tomb-chests may also be canopied in contemporary architectural styles
Medieval tomb-chests may have blind arcading or be carved with weepers, angels or saints or with shields in quatrefoils, etc

Effigies

Before 1500, almost all effigies
were recumbent. The earliest
effigies had legs and hands in
various positions, but after the
mid 14th century legs were
usually rigidly straight and hands
placed together in prayer
Married couples may hold hands
Effigies were rarely portraits of
the dead

Figures carved on tomb-chests
may help to date it. **Weepers**
*(grieving members of the family,
usually offspring)* occurred from
the late 13th century (1); angels
from the late 14th century (2);
and saints in the 15th century (3)

1   2   3

The heads of effigies may be
supported by pillows often held by
angels. A knight's head may rest
on a helmet, his feet against a
couchant lion or other beast
Small figures of **bedesmen** (4)
may be found on a couchant lion's
back and pieces of armour may
appear alongside the effigy

4

Cadavers *(depictions of the
deceased after death)* may occur
alone or in addition to an effigy of
the deceased in life and served as a
memento mori

1550-early 17th century

Renaissance forms and decoration superseded Gothic, characterised by the use of columns, obelisks, strapwork, ribbonwork, grotesques, cherub-heads, allegorical figures etc. Effigy postures were stiff, recumbent, reclining or kneeling at prayer. Demi-figures appeared and, after 1600, sitting or standing figures Roman lettering predominated, although Gothic was still used in the provinces. Effigies were dressed in contemporary costume. Painted and gilded alabaster was very popular. **Notable sculptors**: *Maximilian Colt, Gerard and Nicholas Johnson, William and Cornelius Cure*

Early-mid 17th century

The classical style was now more refined, especially with the use of pediments on architectural canopies and frames; white and black marble competed with alabaster as popular materials. Effigies, mostly in contemporary dress, were found in a variety of poses and were generally less stiff with hands in various positions. Pedestal busts were introduced in this period. Sculptors' signatures were rare until the late 17th century. **Notable sculptors**: *Epiphanius Evesham, Nicholas Stone, Edward and Joshua Marshall, the Christmas family*

c1660-early 18th century

For the baroque tombs of this period, marble superseded alabaster. Recumbent and kneeling effigies were increasingly rare and relief medallion portraits appeared. Costume was usually contemporary but figures may wear Roman armour. Allegorical figures, particularly the Virtues, were common as were symbols of mortality and immortality **Notable sculptors**: *Grinling Gibbons, John Nost, Thomas Green, Caius Gabriel Cibber, John Bushnell, Francis Bird, William and Edward Stanton*

MONUMENTS

MONUMENTS
Floor and wall monuments

18th century

Architectural canopies disappeared after c1750
Black or grey marble as a two-dimensional pyramid
background to standing wall monuments and the
combined use of different coloured marbles on one
monument were popular. All previously mentioned
effigy postures may be found but recumbent and
kneeling were now rare. Figures were often dressed as
Romans, sometimes in armour, sometimes loosely
wrapped in toga-like garments, standing or reclining
on a sarcophagus or against an urn. Small portrait
medallions, busts, putti, urns, cartouches and symbols
of mortality or immortality abounded. Much fine
Rococo decoration is found. **Notable sculptors**:
*Louis Francois Roubiliac, John Michael Rysbrack,
Henry, Peter and Thomas Scheemakers, Henry Cheere,
Joseph Wilton*

Late 18th and early 19th centuries

A more restrained neo-classical style developed,
inspired by ancient Greek models, especially the **stele**
type of design (see page 215). Black and white marble
were still popular, white increasingly so. Recumbent
effigies began a gradual come-back, but very common
in this period was a mourning female leaning over an
urn or sarcophagus. Angels were frequently depicted,
often receiving the deceased at death. Dress was
stylised or contemporary, but naval and military
effigies were often in uniform. **Notable sculptors**:
*Joseph Nollekens, John Bacon and his son John,
Thomas Banks, Richard Westmacott, John Flaxman,
Francis Chantrey, John Francis Moore*

Victorian period

The Greek revival continued, but the
Gothic style enjoyed a massive revival
Black and white marble were still
common but alabaster was revived as a
popular material. The use of canopies was
revived, but particularly popular was the
return of tomb-chests with recumbent
effigies. Reclining, seated and standing
effigies were much rarer. All styles of
lettering were found and the monumental
styles of other periods were sometimes
employed. **Notable sculptors**:
*Peter Hollins, Richard Westmacott the
Younger, Joseph Boehm,
Henry Armstead, Frederick Thrupp*

17th century tablet
Putto on either side of urn
Pedestal bust set in oval niche
Cartouche inscription tablet

Late 18th century tablet
Closed urn
Panel carved in high relief,
curved and angular apron

Cartouche with scrolls, flowers
and drapery, winged cherubs'
heads and an achievement

Mid 20th century rectangular brass tablet
with concave corners. Incised and
black inlaid cursive vine border
Inscription, with flourished capitals,
beginning and ending with a
rubricated patée cross

Stele
background
*(Stele derived
from Greek
memorial slabs
set upright in
the ground)*

Early 19th century symbolism
opium poppies *(the sleep of death)*; sickle
cutting rosebud *(death taking child)*

Lozenge tablet

Square tablet
with clipped,
chamfered or
canted corners
on ground of
conforming
shape

MONUMENTS

215

MONUMENTS
Tomb-chest

15th century tomb-chest

The tomb-chest of Alice, Duchess of Suffolk, d1475. Made of alabaster, it was probably erected soon after her death and stands between the chancel and St John's Chapel.

The tomb-chest stands under a horizontal canopy of panelled stone, with an elaborate cornice of three tiers, the lowest formed of winged demi-figures of angels, each with hands folded on the breast; alternate angels have a crown or tonsure and one wears a fillet with a cross attached. Above the figures is a band of quatrefoils. The uppermost tier consists of elaborate quatrefoil cresting.

The canopy is divided vertically into three equal sections by stone shafts rising from foliated bosses and the capitals crowned with battlements on which stand carved wooden figures, four on each side *(figures should be described)*.

The tomb-chest consists of two tiers and the effigy. On top is the recumbent figure of the Duchess wearing widow's weeds over a contemporary dress *(costume should be described)* with a ducal coronet on her head, a ring on the third finger of the right hand and the Garter on the left forearm. Her hands are closed in prayer and her head rests on a cushion supported by two angels on each side. Above her head is an elaborate canopy carved from a single block of alabaster. At her feet is a lion. Above her feet, on the panelling, is a bracket presumably for the image of a saint.

The side of the tomb-chest, on which the Duchess lies, is carved with a row of canopied niches occupied by frontally standing angels bearing shields with coats of arms. *(Angels should be described and arms blazoned)*. Brass fillets on the cornice of the tomb-chest, on both north and south sides, carry the inscription in black letter in Latin.

Below the chest is an open space, enclosed by an arcade of eight arches on either side, within which may be seen a cadaver clothed in a shroud. On the roof of this compartment, only to be seen by lying on the floor and looking through the arcades, are two paintings, St Mary Magdalene and St John on one side and the Annunciation on the other, a copy of which may be seen on the chancel side of the entrance to the Chapel.

17th century memorial tablet

Rectangular architecturally framed alabaster tablet in memory of Richard Hampden d1662 and his wife Ann d1663

The cream alabaster tablet has a plain black marble border and an inscription incised in roman lettering, capitals and lower case

The marble frame is flanked by white veined, free-standing, angled Ionic columns which support a moulded cornice and segmental pediment with black tympanum, against which, and protruding above, is a carved and painted achievement. The motto is not displayed. *Arms should be blazoned*

Grey marble, acanthus scrolled, tapering wing brackets flank the tablet against the wall

The tablet and columns rest on a black marble shelf supported by black and white erect consoles, between which, set against the wall, is a carved shield with painted coat of arms. *Arms should be blazoned.* Sculptor's name NONE incised on right edge of shelf

18th century memorial tablet

Sarcophagus with a putto sitting at each end of lid, one holding staff with cap of liberty, the other a scroll inscribed Magna Charta. In the centre of the lid is an acanthus spray with ribands stretching to the putti

Directly above is an oval bas-relief with riband cresting and moulded frame, depicting an oak tree hung with coloured shields of Hampdens and allied families, rising from a scene of Chalgrove battlefield (where the parliamentarian, John Hampden, was mortally wounded in 1643)

On the front of the sarcophagus is an inscription in roman lettering, capitals and lower case, straight and slanting, relating to John Hampden d1754 and his descent from John Hampden (above). On the apron, between scrolled and acanthus decorated consoles and with an acanthus spray below the curved and angular lower edge, is the dedication in the same lettering. Only the shields are painted. *Arms should be blazoned*

MONUMENTS
Wall monument

18th century standing wall monument

Large standing wall monument to Henry Petty, 1st Earl of Shelburne and his family in Roman dress.

The monument has a broad base with slightly projecting pedestal-like ends, bearing a large sarcophagus of grey marble, upon which reclines the effigy of the Earl in Roman tunic and toga, with the reclining figure of his wife holding an open book in her left hand. The front of the sarcophagus bears a portrait medallion of Sir William Petty, the Earl's father and founder of the family.

On each side of the monument there is a pair of composite unfluted columns supporting a broken triangular pediment, upon the apex of which is a garlanded urn. Upon one side reclines the figure of Justice and on the other, Truth. Below the feet of each is an urn. Under the arch of the pediment is an heraldic achievement carved in relief. *Arms should be blazoned.* Immediately below, against a tapering back panel swathed in drapery, are two putti among clouds holding a wreath over the head of the expiring nobleman.

Standing upon the pedestal on the dexter side stands the figure of the Earl's son James (died aged 40) dressed in Roman armour and robes. By his side sits his wife (died aged 32) with their son on her lap (died as an infant).

On the sinister side of the pedestal are two female figures in Roman dress and that of a young boy standing between them. These are the daughters of the Earl, Julia and Anne, who died aged 23 and 30, and the Earl's son Charles who died aged 12. The monument is made entirely of marble, the sarcophagus, columns, arch of variously coloured marble and the 12 life-sized figures of white marble. There is a long inscription in the centre of the base incised in roman lettering, capitals and lower case. The monument is enclosed by iron railings erected in 1755.

218

The fashion for brass rubbing has re-awakened interest in memorial brasses, many of which have survived in country churches in fine detail and represent an intriguing picture of the people they commemorate. Brasses were used for both secular and religious characters.

Most memorial brasses date from the 13th to 16th centuries, but there are some impressive 19th century ones, mostly ecclesiastical. The majority have figures as well as inscriptions; these are of great interest for accurate detail of costume, and should be fully described. Dress is of three kinds: civilian, military, ecclesiastical. Good reference books, such as Haines *(see FURTHER READING)*, will provide descriptions and vocabulary for contemporary costume, armour, and vestments. There may be several other elements set in one stone slab: inscriptions on plate, scrolls, or border fillet, groups of children, shields or badges. Some or all of these elements may be missing; in that case describe the shape and position of the indents from which they have gone. A rubbing taken of the brass can often be photographed more successfully than the brass itself.

Casement	slab into which a brass is set
Indent or matrix	mark left in casement by missing brass
Latten	alloy of copper and zinc with lead and tin used in the making of brasses
Palimpsest	old brasses re-engraved on the reverse side

15th century memorial brass (see page 220)
Memorial to Sir William Colwell, d1443. Floor, centre of S aisle
Two figures are set beneath crocketed ogee arches of a double canopy with embattled entablature and pinnacled and buttressed shafting. Four shields of arms in a row between the arches and the entablature. *Arms should be blazoned.*

In a roundel within the man's canopy is a rebus device: a collet over a well. The roundel on the woman's side is blank. A Latin inscription in gothic lettering runs across the foot of the main panel, below this two groups of children, the girls on the left below their mother, the sons below the father. Surrounding all a border strip with roundels at the corners containing the emblems of the Evangelists; this has fragments of a marginal inscription, also in Latin in gothic letters, much of it now missing. Two prayer scrolls curving above the figures' heads contain inscriptions, in the same style of lettering.

The man, on the right, is bare-headed, with **bowl-crop** hair. He wears full plate armour including gauntlets and sabatons, sword and dagger. His feet, with rowel spurs, rest on a lion. His lady wears a heart-shaped headdress with short veil, a high-waisted houppelande with v-neck and long wide sleeves over an undergown with full sleeves gathered close at the wrist. A little dog nestles at her feet. The four daughters kneel, dressed like their mother. The four sons stand, and wear full-skirted gowns. All figures have their hands clasped in prayer.

Slab l. 94cm x w. 44cm; h. of main figures 40cm

Entablature

Finial

Pinnacle

Coat of arms

Crocket

Double canopy

Rebus

Canopy pediment

Prayer scroll

Knight

Wife

Canopy shafting

Marginal inscription

Footrest

Foot inscription

Sons

Daughters

Symbol of Evangelist

MUSICAL INSTRUMENTS
Working instruments

Apart from keyboards and barrel organs, it is unusual to find working instruments in churches today. No working instrument should be handled without permission and supervision. Occasionally instruments used in 18th and 19th century church bands may survive. Always enquire about these.

Organ	see page 226
Chamber organ	free standing, small instruments described in the same way as organs
Barrel organ	mechanical instruments which often resemble chamber organs. Pipes worked off large pinned barrels (like those of a musical box) turned by a handle. Name of maker, number of stops, number of barrels and list of tunes of each barrel are of interest Not all tunes may be hymns and sacred airs. Some barrel organs can also be played manually
Carillon	bells struck from a form of keyboard and/or from pinned barrels. Located in church tower. Note the number of bells, name of bell founder and repertoire on any barrels
Piano	either winged, like a grand piano, or upright. Name of maker to be found on board above the keys. Note any special features like candle brackets or more than two pedals

CHURCH BANDS

The instruments most commonly used to accompany church choirs in the 18th and 19th centuries were:

Flute, flageolet, clarinet or oboe
simple tubes, probably in boxwood with a minimum of keys, usually for the little finger. Look for the name of the maker and serial number.

Serpent, ophecleide, bassoon or bass horn
low sounding instruments with long tubes, some curly (**serpent**) or folded (**bassoon**). Look for the name of the maker and serial number.

Key bugle or trombone
brass instruments, the bugle with padded keys; the trombone in two sections, one of which can be slid to and fro to lengthen or shorten the tubing and thus produce lower and higher sounding notes. The name of the maker may be stamped or engraved on the bell.

Violin, cello or double bass
The name of the maker and other information may be on a label visible with a torch shone through the sound holes. In case these happen to be very early examples, take line drawings or photographs. Proportions of neck to fiddle and other details may indicate the date of the instrument. Note if the stringing is of gut or wire or both.

Pitchpipe
used to give the choir 'the note'.

INSTRUMENTS SEEN IN CARVING, STAINED GLASS AND PAINTINGS
No detail is too tiny to be noted in line drawings or photographs. The variety of early musical instruments is so bewildering that it is often difficult to identify one example accurately. Even then, different names are sometimes given to the same instrument.
Drawings and photographs should therefore make clear the following:
how the instrument is held; number of strings on bowed and plucked instruments; precise position and shape of any sound holes; number of finger holes on wind instruments; their precise position and keys.

MUSICAL INSTRUMENTS
Stringed instruments played with a bow

Rebeck
*(long neck, pearshaped
body, arched back);*
played under chin

Violin

Double bass
*(similar to cello but larger,
with end pin),*
played from behind

Tromba marina

Cello
played between knees

Viol
played between knees

MUSICAL INSTRUMENTS
Plucked instruments

Lute

Cittern
(fig-shaped, 4/5 metal strings) played with a plectrum

Medieval harp

Lyre

Psaltery
(strings horizontal above soundboard)

Pedal harp
(harp strings vertical to the soundboard)

MUSICAL INSTRUMENTS
Wind instruments

Recorder   **Shawm**   **Crumhorn**   **Bassoon**   **Cornett**

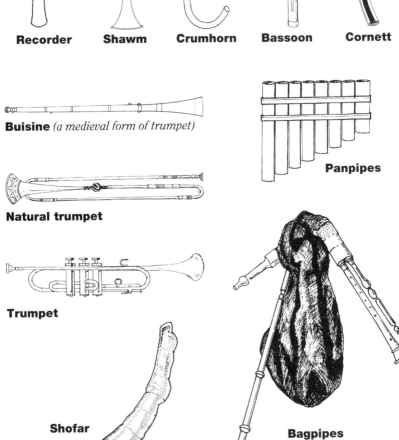

Buisine *(a medieval form of trumpet)*

Natural trumpet

Panpipes

Trumpet

Shofar

Bagpipes

MUSICAL INSTRUMENTS
Percussion and keyboard instruments

Portative organ

Tabor

Pipe and tabor

Organistrum or hurdy-gurdy

KEYBOARD

Cottage piano small upright piano with iron frame introduced by Robert Wornum in 1813. Other makers include Southwell, William Allen, Stodart, Alphaeus Babcock, Conrad Mayer and Jonas Chickering

Harmonium small free reed keyboard instrument invented in 1840. Good examples made by the Paris firm of Alexandre, Pere & Fils

Electronic organ instruments in which the sound is generated often by sophisticated electronic means which is amplified and played through loud speakers. These are either mounted within the instrument or more usually placed separately within the building. An early example of the type by Hammond was popular for a time but there are now very few of these left

Pianola automatic piano player driven by foot pedals played from perforated rolls, developed between 1887-1897

Piano either grand or upright. A trade label may give the name of the maker. Some best known makers are Erard, Broadwood, Bechstein, Steinway, Clementi

Portative organ small portable organs made from the 12th to mid 17th centuries. They were played by one person, who operated the bellows with the left hand and the keys with the right hand

Positive organ chamber organs designed for church or home use; a second person operated the bellows

MUSICAL INSTRUMENTS
Organs

Since the middle ages, or even before, church music has been associated with the organ and perhaps a zenith of the art of organ building was reached in the late 17th and 18th centuries. None of these instruments survive in original form but the restoring zeal of the Victorians provided the majority of British churches with an organ which often is one of the dominant features of the building.

The most important 19th century organ builders were Hill, Willis, Gray and Davison and Walker but architects often had a hand in the design of cases to house them and examples by Pugin, Scott, Pearson and Bodley exist. A plate on the console will often reveal the name of the builder unless this has been replaced in later restoration work. It is harder to tell whether an organ is original to the building or has been removed from elsewhere.

It is rare that an organ of earlier date than 1840 survives, but occasionally parts have been incorporated into a later instrument. Early instruments usually have a note other than C as their lowest note.

Cornice	
Pipe shades	
Pipe flats	
Casework	
Pipe tower	
Impost	
Stopknobs	
Manual keys	
Pedal keys	

Case	the wood frame in which and behind which the pipes sit, which varies from a simple rack to a grand piece of furniture with a cornice and other embellishments
Console	where the player sits with manual and pedal keyboards
Flats	flat groups of pipes in the case
Jambs	panels for the stops at the side of the keyboards which may be set at an angle
Pipeshades	decorated features usually of carved wood, filling the gap between the sloping line of pipe tops and the frame of the case

Stops or stopknobs	knobs which control pitch and tone mounted at the side on the jambs with ivory or plastic heads to indicate their function Alternatively the stops may be in the form of ivory or plastic tabs set above the keyboards
Towers	groups of pipes which often project forward at the sides and/or centre of the case, usually containing taller and fewer pipes than in the flats

PIPES

Organ pipes are made of wood or metal, wood being common for the largest pipes. Metal pipes are often made of zinc but an alloy of tin and lead is better for tone. Where the tin content is high they may have a mottled appearance known as **spotted metal**. The front pipes are few in number and made for show so that they may be highly decorative, painted with diapered patterns. Most of the pipes will be out of sight inside the body of the case.

ACTION

Organs produce sound when wind is allowed to enter the pipes which stand vertically on and resonate against a rectangular chest or **soundboard** within the body of the organ. There are four types of action of which **mechanical** is the simplest form; indeed the musical value of this system has now been realised by most players and many new instruments use mechanical action.

Mechanical or tracker action	player directly controls the entry of wind into the pipes by a system of levers which open the valves called **pallets**
Pneumatic action	player's action conveyed by an air pressure system, identifiable by the presence of large amounts of small bore lead tubing inside the lower parts of the case; a popular system from 1880 to 1930
Electro-pneumatic action	a modification of pneumatic action in which the primary energising of the entry of wind into the pipes is controlled by small electro-magnets
Direct electric action	entry of wind into the pipes is controlled electrically by solenoids

CONSOLE

The console will have at least one row of keys or manual and usually a row of pedal keys. Organs may have one to four manuals and even, very rarely, five. Each of the keyboards has a particular name and groups of stops relate to each.

Great organ	the only manual or the lowest of two
Swell organ	the upper of two or three manuals
Choir organ	the lowest of three manuals
Solo organ	the upper manual above the swell in organs with more than three manuals
Pedal organ	the sound is controlled by the pedal keys

Record details of materials and appearance; makers' name plate; any visible signs of repair; any evidence of maintenance (tuner's notebook); lowest and highest notes of each keyboard

WINDOWS
Terms

Since the introduction of stained glass in the 12th century the windows of a church have often been its chief glory. In the Middle Ages they were richly coloured storybooks. In spite of the iconoclasts, fine examples survive and re-assembled fragments are preserved in many churches. By the 16th century heraldic glass was important. In the 17th the religious climate condemned painted windows, much of what is to be found from that time is imported.

The 18th century designers used enamelling and treated windows as huge paintings. In the 19th century glaziers rediscovered the medieval tradition, and there was a splendid renaissance in stained and painted glass. With the vast increase in the number of churches in the second half of the century there was much stereotyped work, but the brilliant innovations of the Pre-Raphaelites, and those whom they inspired, gave an impetus which lasted into this century and which has produced its own idioms, including much abstract work.

Some glaziers signed their windows or included a maker's mark (see page 235). Others did not, but certain workshops can be recognised by their use of standard models such as angels, monograms and border motifs. Symbols and allegory play a large part, particularly with figures of saints or biblical scenes, and the iconography of pictorial windows is a fascinating study. *(See ATTRIBUTES & ALLEGORY pages 12-29 and FURTHER READING).*

Texts and inscriptions are of two kinds: quotations, mostly scriptural; and commemorative or dedicatory inscriptions. The latter may be within the window or somewhere nearby.

The stonework frame of the window is usually in one of a series of well-defined Gothic styles, either original or reproduced, often with a number of minor lights in the upper tracery; these may also portray figures or small scenes related to the subject of the main lights. Windows without coloured glass usually consist of clear or tinted quarries *(small lozenge-shaped panes)*. They may however be leaded in complex geometric patterns, using glass of several pale shades.

Blind tracery	areas with blank stone or other infill, not glass
Calm	see **leading**
Canopy	framework either architectural (arches, turrets, pillars, etc) or foliate around the figures contained in the lights
Cusp	projecting point between foils
Dedication	commemoration message for donor or event
Enamelling	*See METAL: Terms (page 101)*
Eyelets	smallest elements in tracery
Ferramenta	metal window grid formed of vertical and occasionally horizontal bars to which the glazing is attached
Fillets	narrow glass borders next to stonework frame
Foil	concave element in stonework, between cusps; heads of arches are often trefoil or cinquefoil, tracery lights may be of any number of foils

Grisaille	monochromatic patterns on clear glass in yellow, grey, or brown, used from 13th century and copied in 19th and 20th centuries (see also **Stamped quarries**)
Hachures	small shading lines
Heraldic	containing coats of arms
Inscription	**Memoria**l: to persons, family or group or **commemorative**: of event or institution
Leading	framing of individual pieces of glass with lead calms of H-section, usually outlining each area of one colour
Lights	sections of window divided by transoms or mullions
Lined out	outlined in black paint or enamel
Quarries	small regular diamond-shaped panes; any with horizontal and vertical leading are called **square quarries**
Stained glass	common term for coloured glass; shading is added by painting and other techniques. (see also **Silver stain**)
Silver stain	the only glass which is truly stained, by either silver sulphide or chloride, to produce various shades of yellow glass; process discovered in the early 14th century
Stamped quarries	19th century process for mass production of quarries decorated with a monochrome motif
Tracery	ornamental shapes formed by the branching of mullions in the upper part of a window
Texts	quotations from Bible or other sources
Tracery lights	sections of the ornamental tracery formed by the branching of mullions in the upper part of a window

Oriel
when supported on corbels

Lucarne
on a spire

Dormer
on a house roof

Lunette
semi-circular window, panel or decoration

Wheel window
round window with radiating tracery

Rose window
round window with concentric tracery

Note the sequence in which round window lights should be numbered

WINDOWS

WINDOWS
Types

Saxon and Norman (Romanesque) windows were small and usually unglazed. This was for security and because of limited building knowledge. Builders did not dare to weaken the wall with large openings. English glass-making largely died out after the departure of the Romans and imports from France and Germany were costly. During the Middle Ages building confidence grew, times were less troubled, windows became larger. Arch heads followed the Gothic pattern (see pages 8-9). Tracery designs are illustrated on pages 231-2.

With the return of classicism the Renaissance windows were round-headed, for example, Sir Christopher Wren's 17th century churches. He also used the circular **oeil de boeuf** form as did Baroque architects of the early 18th century. With the 19th century Gothic Revival, the pointed arch and coloured glass were once more designed, a pattern which continued well into the 20th century.

Saxon window openings

Norman (Romanesque) window

Wren oeil de boeuf (bull's eye) window 1670-80

Wren window, 1685

Rose window, Pearson, 1875

Baroque oeil de boeuf window, 1712

Lancet window, 1845

Maufe Cathedral window, 1939

Drawings by Doreen Yarwood

Tracery is the term used to describe the varied forms of stone and glass decoration of the window head during the Middle Ages. The earliest window lights (see page 230) which evolved after the Gothic introduction of the pointed arch (see pages 8-9) were single lancets. These were narrow, undecorated lights. Soon it became customary to group the lancets (3, 5 or 7) under one arch moulding. The next stage was to create a single window under the encompassing arch which would be divided vertically by mullions. The solid stone head was pierced by cut out shapes: this was **plate tracery**. From this derived **bar tracery** where the glass area became greater and the stonework narrower. Windows grew steadily larger and were divided by a greater number of vertical mullions and horizontal transoms. Designs of the head developed from reticulated (**net**) forms, to geometrical, curvilinear (**flowing lines**) and finally to the panel (**perpendicular**) types. Each part of the design was shaped in small arcs of stone called **foils**. The number of foils were indicated by the prefix: trefoil (3); quatrefoil (4); cinquefoil (5) or multifoil (many). The points of the foils are called **cusps**. Circular windows were common. These were decoratively traceried. The early types were **plate tracery wheel windows**; these had radiating spokes. Later came the **rose window** with geometric or curvilinear tracery.

Quatrefoil

Trefoils

Wheel window
1440

Geometrical tracery
1260-80

Cusp

Plate tracery
1250

Curvilinear tracery c1350

Grouped lancets c1200

Panel (perpendicular)
tracery 1485-1509

WINDOWS
Tracery

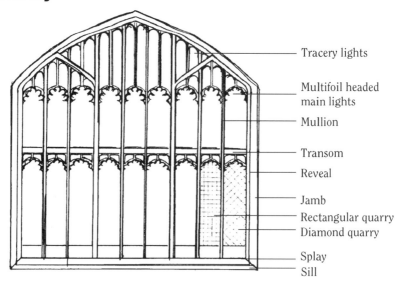

Tracery lights

Multifoil headed main lights

Mullion

Transom

Reveal

Jamb

Rectangular quarry
Diamond quarry

Splay
Sill

Window of nine multifoiled lights, arranged in triplets in two stages with tracery of 15th century rectilinear form

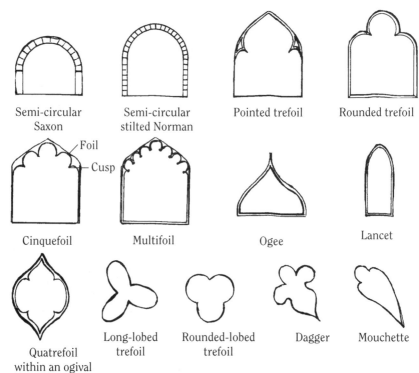

Semi-circular
Saxon

Semi-circular
stilted Norman

Pointed trefoil

Rounded trefoil

Foil

Cusp

Cinquefoil

Multifoil

Ogee

Lancet

Quatrefoil
within an ogival

Long-lobed
trefoil

Rounded-lobed
trefoil

Dagger

Mouchette

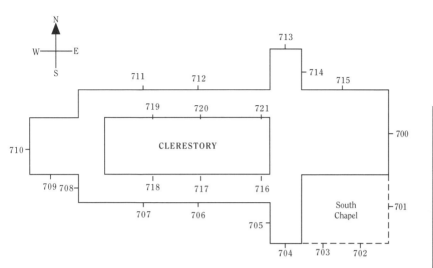

Number the windows clockwise from the E window (700) all round the ground floor, including porches and vestries. Then clockwise again round any clerestory, and finally the upper stories of the tower. Number a plan of the church to show positions of all windows. (Sections of the church, such as chapels, should be labelled with the names used by the congregation).

Aim to have a number of photographs of each window, or type of window. Windows with tracery lights should have a diagram on the same page as their description, with the lights numbered from left to right and top to bottom. Sections of the descripion are then identified by these numbers, shown in brackets. (To avoid confusion with the format nos 1 to 10).

Follow the arrangements shown in sample pages and page 234. Having described the stonework in general terms, proceed to describe shape and contents of tracery lights. For pictorial windows, preface the description of the individual main lights with the name of the subject (if spread over all lights), and describe any elements common to all lights, (eg background, borders, angels, scrolls).

Give the words of bible quotations, etc, as you come to them in the description. If the source is given, make it clear whether that was in the window or is your research. Commemorative inscriptions have their text quoted at 9. Do not forget to record any identifying glaziers' marks, signatures etc, preferably accompanied by sketch or photograph.

Close-up colour photographs of important elements of a window greatly enhance the Record, and may replace some of the descriptive text otherwise necessary. Remember to quote all references and sources.

WINDOWS
Late 19th century window

Stonework	Late 19th century, three trefoil headed lights and seven traceries in 14th century reticulated style

Tracery Lights

1	Dove descending amidst three stars in purple night sky
2 and 3	Sprig of oak leaves with acorn in natural colouring against a light yellow ground
4	Crescent moon against dark blue sky
5	Sun against light blue sky
6 and 7	A trefoil lined out in black against a pale yellow ground
Main Lights	Adoration of the Shepherds and the Magi
8, 9 and 10	In each a group of three angels with multicoloured wings and wearing white girdled tunics. Each central angel playing a musical instrument, rebeck, harp and tabor respectively, outer ones all singing
11, 12 and13	Text in gothic capitals and lower case, painted in black on a pale yellow ground. It is difficult to decipher but enough to identify with Matt 2: *We have seen his star/in the East and are come/to adore him*
14	Three shepherds, placed vertically, upper two standing, one kneeling, all wear nomads' head-dresses, each in a different brightly coloured cloak, red, yellow and blue; two hold crooks, the kneeling shepherd does not appear to have one
15	Virgin Mary seated with infant Christ on her knee, Joseph standing behind. Virgin wears a royal blue mantel with gold trimming. Infant Christ swaddled. Joseph wears a dark red cloak over a long green tunic. The Virgin and Joseph each have a yellow nimbus, the Christ child has a yellow and white cruciform nimbus
16	Three Magi similarly placed to the shepherds: Caspar in purple robe with fur cape-collar attached with a tied cord; Melchior in rich brown robe; Balthazar, the youngest kneeling and bearing a gift, wears a white tunic and emerald green super-tunic, with his crown on the ground in front of him
	Plain white dado behind all three scenes, band of light blue sky above
17 and 19	A kneeling angel dressed in a white robe, with flame coloured wings and nimbus, yellow stain seaweed background
18	Old Testament Altar of Sacrifice in natural colours against a green ground
20	Artist's signature. Mark of a daisy within a bell: Margaret Bell

Reginald
Bell

Clayton & Bell

Clayton & Bell

John Clement
Bell

Alfred Bell

M C Farrar
Bell

William Wailes

C C Townshend
& J Howson

Goddard
& Gibbs

Rachel de
Montmorency

Hugh
Easton

Horace
Wilkinson

J W Kubler

E F
Brickdale

Edward
Jenkins
Prest

WINDOWS
Makers' marks

H W Bryans

J N Comper

Pope & Parr

Martin Travers

A R Fisher

T Willement

J N Lawson

J E Nuttgens

Chapel Studios

Caroline Benyon

Percy Bacon & Bros

Lawrence S Lee

J Wippell & Co Exeter pre-1970 and 1980-present

Wippell Mowbray Church Furnishing Ltd 1970-1980

Ray Bradley

Henry James Salisbury

N H J Westlake

Tom Carter Shapland

H J Stammers

A C W Younger

Robert Hendra and
Geoffrey Harper

Moira Forsyth

K Parsons Paul Woodroffe

H W Harvey

Martin Webb

Powell & Sons
of Whitefriars

Christopher
Webb

Geoffrey Webb

C E Kempe
pre 1907

C E Kempe & Co Ltd
1907-1934

Francis
Skeat

Francis
Skeat

W Holland
Warwick

William
Warrington

M E Aldrich
Rope

J C
Bewsey

FURTHER READING

Inside Churches can be no more than an introduction to the decoration and furnishings encountered in British churches. In each subject area there are many helpful secondary sources, some of which are recommended here. Some interesting primary sources may also be available through the incumbent of the parish or through county record offices.

Recognised Church Recorders may also refer queries to various professionals through the National Association of Decorative and Fine Arts Societies.

General Reading

Addleshaw, G W O and Etchells, Frederick
The Architectural Setting of Anglican Worship
Faber and Faber, 1948

Anson, Peter
Fashions in Church Furnishings, 1840-1940
Faith Press, 1960

Betjeman, Sir John
Collins Guide to Parish Churches of England and Wales
Collins, 1980

Burman, Peter (ed)
Treasures on Earth
Donhead Pub Ltd, 1994 and 1997

Clowmay, Paul and Tessa
Exploring Churches
Lion Publishing, 1993

Cox, Charles and Harvey, Alfred
English Church Furniture
E P Publishing, 1973

Elrington, Christopher (ed)
The Victoria History of the Counties of England
Oxford University Press

Howkins, Christopher
Discovering Church Furniture
Shire Publications, 1980

Lewis, Philippa and Darley, Gillian
Dictionary of Ornament
Macmillan, 1986

Miller, Judith (ed)
Miller's Pocket Antiques Fact File
Mitchell Beazley, 1988

Pevsner, Sir Nikolaus and others
The Buildings of England
Penguin

Randall, Gerald
Church Furnishing and Decoration in England and Wales
Batsford, 1980

Robinson, John Martin
Treasures of the English Churches
Sinclair Stevenson, 1995

Royal Commission on the Historical Monuments of England
Inventories of Historical Monuments
HMSO

Stafford, Maureen and Ware, Dora
An Illustrated Dictionary of Ornament
Allen and Unwin, 1974

Victoria and Albert Museum
Victorian Church Art
Exhibition catalogue (November 1971-January 1972)

Architecture

Child, Mark	**Discovering Church Architecture** *Shire Publications, 1976*
Council for British Archaeology	**Recording a Church: An Illustrated Glossary** *1996* ISBN 1 872414 567
Curl, James Stevens	**English Architecture: An Illustrated Glossary** *David and Charles, 1987* ISBN 0 71538 8878
Fletcher, Sir Bannister	**History of Architecture** *Athlone Press, 1975*
Harries, John	**Discovering Churches** *Shire Publications, 1972*
Harris, John and Lever, Jill	**Illustrated Glossary of Architecture 850-1830** *Faber and Faber, 1966, 1993* ISBN 0 571 13766 0 Pbk
Yarwood, Doreen	**Encyclopaedia of Architecture** *Batsford*

Attributes & Allegory

Child, Heather and Colles, Dorothy	**Christian Symbols, Ancient and Modern** *Bell and Hyman, 1971*
Farmer, David Hugh	**The Oxford Dictionary of Saints** *Oxford University Press, 1978*
Ferguson, George	**Signs and Symbols in Christian Art** *Galaxy Books, London 1996*
Hall, James	**Dictionary of Subjects and Symbols in Art** *John Murray, 1987* ISBN 0 7195 4147 6
Hulme, Edward F	**Symbolism in Christian Art** *Allen and Unwin, London 1910*
Post, Ellwood W	**Saints, Signs and Symbols** *SPCK, 1964*

Costume

Borg, Alan	**Arms and Armour in Britain** *HMSO, 1977*
Blair, Claude	**European and American Arms c1100-1850** *Batsford, 1962*
Mayo, Janet	**The History of Ecclesiastical Dress** *Batsford, 1985*
Cunnington, Pamela	**A Dictionary of English Costume** *A and C Black, 1960*
Cunnington, Pamela	**Handbook of English Costume (various volumes)** *Faber and Faber, 1973*
Yarwood, Doreen	**English Costume from the 2nd Century BC to 1960** *Batsford*

Decoration

Brackett, O	**English Furniture Illustrated** *Hamlyn*
Croft-Murray, Edward	**Decorative Mural Painting in England, 1537-1837** *Country Life, 1962*

Croft-Murray, Edward	**Decorative Painting in England, the 18th and 19th Centuries**
	Country Life, 1970
Gloag, John	**A Short Dictionary of Furniture**
	Allen and Unwin, 1952
Meyer, F S	**Handbook of Ornament**
	Dover, 1957
Rouse, Clive	**Medieval Wall Paintings**
	Shire Publications, 1991
Ware, Dora and	**An Illustrated Dictionary of Ornament**
Stafford, M	*Allen and Unwin, 1974*

Heraldry

Brooke-Little, John (ed)	**Boutell's Heraldry**
	F Warne, 1978
Brooke-Little, John	**Royal Heraldry**
	Pilgrim Press, 1981
Burke, Sir John Bernard	**The General Armory of England, Scotland, Ireland and Wales**
	Tabard, 1966
Frear, Jacqueline	**Discovering Heraldry**
	Shire Publications, 1983 ISBN 0 85263 4765
Fox-Davies, Arthur Charles	**A Complete Guide to Heraldry**
	Nelson, 1969
Friar, Stephen	**A New Dictionary of Heraldry**
	Alpha Books, 1987
MacKinnon, Charles	**The Observer Book of Heraldry**
	F Warne
Moncrieffe, Sir Iain and	**Simple Heraldry Cheerfully Illustrated**
Pottinger, Don	*Nelson, 1952*
Papworth, John Wood	**Papworth's Ordinary of British Armorials**
	Tabard, 1961
Storry, J G	**Church Heraldry**
	Nettlebed Press, 1983
Summers, Peter	**Hatchments in Britain (Volumes 1-10)**
	Phillimore, 1974-1980

Lettering

Johnston, E	**Writing and Illuminating and Lettering**
	Pitman, 1906
Macklin, Rev Herbert	**The Brasses of England**
	E P Group, 1975
Stribling M (compiler)	**The Calligraphy Source Book**
	Macdonald

Ceramics

Barnard, Julian	**Victorian Ceramic Tiles**
	Studio Vista, 1972
Cushion, John P	**A Handbook of Pottery and Porcelain Marks**
and Honey, W B	*Faber and Faber*
Eames, Elizabeth S	**English Medieval Tiles**
	British Museum, 1985

Eames, Elizabeth S	**Medieval Craftsmen: English Tilers**
	British Museum, 1992
Fawcett, Jane (ed)	**Historic Floors: Their History and**
	Conservation
	Butterworth Heinemann, Oxford, 1998
Hughes, G Bernard	**The Country Life Collectors' Pocket Book**

Metal

Bambery, Anneke	**Old Sheffield Plate**
	Shire Publications, 1988 ISBN 0 85263 965 1
Banister, Judith (ed)	**English Silver Hallmarks**
	Foulsham, 1970, 1983
Camp, John	**Discovering Bells and Bellringing**
	Shire Publications, 1997 ISBN 0 85263 290 8
Cotterell, Howard Herschel	**Old Pewter, Its Makers and Marks**
	C E Tuttle, 1963
Council for British Archaeology	**Fixtures and Fittings in Dated Houses 1567-1765**
Emmerson, Robin	**Church Plate**
	Church House Pub. 1991
Hollister-Short, G J	**Discovering Wrought Iron**
	Shire Publications, 1970
Hull, Charles	**Pewter**
	Shire Publications, 1992 ISBN 0 7478 0152 5
Oman, Charles	**English Church Plate**
	Oxford University Press, 1957
Peal, Christopher	**British Pewter and Britannia Metal**
	John Gifford, 1971
Pickford, Ian (ed)	**Jackson's Silver and Gold Marks of England, Scotland and Ireland from 1300-1850**
	Antique Collectors Club, 1989
Pickford, Ian (ed)	**Jackson's Hallmarks Pocket ed. English, Scottish and Irish Silver and Gold Marks, from 1300-1991**
	Antique Collectors Club, 1991
Walters, H B	**Church Bells of England**
	Oxford University Press, 1977

Paper

Briquet, Charles M	**Les Filigranes**
	Paris, 1907
Darley, L S	**Introduction to Book Binding**
	Faber and Faber, 1965
Heawood, Edward	**Watermarks etc**
	1950
Tate, W E	**The Parish Chest: A Study of the Records of Parochial Administration in England**
	Cambridge University Press, 1969, 1983

Stone

| Bond, Francis | **Fonts and Font Covers** |
| | *Waterstone, 1985* |

Kilburn, Father E	**A Walk Around the Church of the London Oratory**
	Sand and Co, 1966
Pounds, Norman	**Church Fonts**
	Shire Publications, 1995

Textiles

Earnshaw, Pat	**The Identification of Lace**
	Shire Publications, 1984
Dean, Beryl	**Ecclesiastical Embroidery**
	Batsford, 1958
Dean, Beryl	**Embroidery in Religion and Ceremonial**
	Batsford, 1981
Fokker, Nicolas	**Persian and Other Oriental Carpets for Today**
	Allen and Unwin, 1973
Hands, Hinda	**Church Needlework**
	Faith Press, 1957
Kelly, Francis M and Schwabe, Randolph	**A Short History of Costume and Armour, 1066-1800**
	David and Charles, 1972
Norris, H	**Church Vestments: Their Origin and Development**
	Dent and Son, 1949
Schoester, Mary	**The Watts Book of Embroidery**
	Watts and Co, 1998

Wood

Chinnery, Victor	**Oak Furniture: The British Tradition**
	Antique Collectors Club, 1988
Council for British Archaeology	**Recording Timber-framed Buildings**
	ISBN 1 872414 729
Corkhill, Thomas	**A Glossary of Wood**
	Stobart and Sons, 1984
Edwards, R	**A Shorter Dictionary of English Furniture**
	Hamlyn, 1964
Gloag, John	**A Short Dictionary of Furniture**
	Allen and Unwin, 1952
Hayman, Richard	**Church Misericords & Bench Ends**
	Shire Publications, 1989
Hayward, C H	**English Period Furniture**
	Evans, 1971
Hewett, Cecil A	**Church Carpentry**
	Unwin Brothers Ltd, 1982
Howard, F E and Crossley, Frederick H	**English Church Woodwork**
	Batsford, 1927
Jervis, Simon	**The Woodwork of Winchester Cathedral**
	Friends of Winchester Cathedral, 1976
Joy, E T	**The Country Life Book of Chairs**
	Hamlyn, 1967
Smith, J C D	**A Guide to Woodcarving: Misericords and Bench-ends**
	David and Charles, 1974

Smith, J C D	**Church Woodcarving: A West Country Study**
	David and Charles, 1969
Tracy, Charles	**English Medieval Furniture and Woodwork**
	Victoria and Albert Museum, 1990

Clocks

Baillie, G H	**Watchmakers and Clockmakers of the World**
	NAG Press, 1976 Volume I
Beeson, C F C	**English Church Clocks, 1280-1850**
	Phillimore, 1971
Betts, J	**The National Trust Pocket Guide to Clocks**
	Octopus, 1985
Loomes, Brian	**Watchmakers and Clockmakers of the World**
	NAG Press, 1976 Volume II
McKay, Chris	**The Turret Keeper's Handbook**
	Antiquarian Horological Society, 1998
	ISBN 0 901180 327
Rose, R E	**English Dial Clocks**
	Antique Collectors Club, 1978
Smith, A	**Clocks and Watches**
	1975

Memorials and Monuments

Bertram, Jerome Fr (ed)	**Monumental Brasses: As Art and History**
	Alan Sutton Publishing Ltd, 1996
Chapman, Leigh	**Brasses and Brass Rubbing**
	Shire Publications, 1987
Esdaile, Kathleen	**English Church Monuments, 1510-1840**
	Batsford, 1946
Greenhill, Frank	**Incised Effigal Slabs**
	Faber and Faber, 1976
Haines, Herbert	**A Manual of Monumental Brasses**
	1861
Kemp, Brian	**English Church Monuments**
	Batsford, 1988
Kemp, Brian	**Church Monuments**
	Shire Publications, 1988
Macklin, Rev Herbert	**The Brasses of England**
	EP Group, 1975
Meara, David	**Victorian Memorial Brasses**
	Routledge & Kegan Paul, 1983
Mill Stephenson, B A	**A List of Monumental Brasses in the British Isles**
	Headley, 1926
Norris, Malcolm	**Monumental Brasses: The Craft**
	Faber and Faber, 1978
Norris, Malcolm	**Monumental Brasses: The Memorials**
	Phillips and Page, 1989
Stone, Lawrence	**Sculpture in Britain: The Middle Ages**
	Penguin, 1955
Tummers, H A	**Early Secular Effigies in England: The Thirteenth Century**
	Brill, 1980

Whinney, Margaret	**Sculpture in Britain: 1530-1830** *Penguin, 1964*

Musical Instruments

Baker, David	**The Organ** *Shire Publications, 1991*
Clutton, Cecil and Niland, Austin	**The British Organ** *Batsford, 1963*
Hindley, G	**Musical Instruments** *Hamlyn, 1971*
Remnant, Mary	**Musical Instruments - An illustrated history** *Batsford, 1989*

Windows

Archer, Michael	**An Introduction to English Stained Glass** *HMSO, 1985*
Hall, James	**Dictionary of Subjects and Symbols in Art** *Murray, 1989*
Harrison, Kenneth	**An Illustrated Guide to the Windows of King's College Chapel, Cambridge** *Cambridge University Press, 1953*
Harrison, Martin	**Victorian Stained Glass** *Barrie and Jenkins, 1980*
Harries, John	**Discovering Stained Glass** *Shire Publications, 1980*
Kirby, H T	**The Stained Glass Artist** *British Society of Master Glass Painters' Journal Vol X, No 4, 1950-51*
Lee, Lawrence, Seddon, George and Stephens, Francis	**Stained Glass** *Mitchell Beazley, 1976*
Sewter, A Charles	**The Stained Glass of William Morris and His Circle** *Yale University Press, 1974-75*

NOTES